W9-DJE-982

CAREERS

IN SCIENCE

VGM Professional Careers Series

CAREERS
IN SCIENCE

THOMAS A. EASTON

Foreword by
Richard C. Atkinson
President
American Association for the Advancement of Science

VGM Career Horizons
a division of *NTC Publishing Group*
Lincolnwood, Illinois USA

Library of Congress Cataloging-in-Publication Data

Easton, Thomas A.
    Careers in science / Thomas A. Easton.
        p.   cm. -- (VGM professional careers series)
    Bibliography: p.
    Includes index.
    ISBN 0-8442-8693-1: $14.95. -- ISBN 0-8442-8695-8 (pbk.): $9.95
    1. Science--Vocational guidance.   I. Title.   II. Series.
Q147.E27   1989
    502.3--dc20   89-16482
                                                                      CIP

Published by VGM Career Horizons, a division of NTC Publishing Group.
© 1990 by NTC Publishing Group, 4255 West Touhy Avenue,
Lincolnwood (Chicago), Illinois 60646-1975 U.S.A.
9 0 VP 9 8 7 6 5 4 3 2 1

CONTENTS

Undergrad.

ABOUT THE AUTHOR

Thomas A. Easton holds a doctorate in theoretical biology from the University of Chicago and teaches at Thomas College, a small business school, while enjoying life on the Maine Coast. His work on scientific and futuristic issues has appeared in many magazines, from *Astronomy* to *Consumer Reports* and *Robotics Age*. His short stories and poems have also appeared widely.

Dr. Easton is a member of the Science Fiction Writers of America and a well-known science fiction critic, with a monthly book review column in the science fiction magazine *Analog*. His books have dealt not only with careers in science but also with writing, creativity, the privatization of social services, entrepreneurs, consultants, and business auctions. He has also published a science fiction novel, computer software, and biology textbooks.

ACKNOWLEDGMENTS

I wish to thank Tom Hogan, who first enticed me into writing about careers, and my wife, who has long tolerated the financial uncertainties of the writer's career.

Thomas A. Easton

FOREWORD

It is difficult to think of an aspect of modern life that is untouched by the advances of science. We enjoy steaming hot microwave meals that were frozen solid just five minutes earlier. Fax messages are sent from an office in Chicago to Japan in a matter of minutes, increasing the efficiency and productivity of the working world. Rampant diseases that were once deadly are now prevented from occurring with vaccinations. Scientists continue to amaze us with ways of improving our lives, just as they amazed generations of the past with wheels, glass, refrigeration, light bulbs, and penicillin.

The fields of science offer a wide variety of opportunities. Many scientists today work in medicine and health, treating, curing, and preventing illnesses. Others, working in the life, physical, earth, and space sciences, perform invaluable research that contributes to the ever-growing body of knowledge. Engineers and computer scientists work for industry, designing and building devices that make life easier and more comfortable. Others devote their lives to educating tomorrow's scientists. While scientists can be found in many different settings, working at a broad spectrum of jobs, their goal remains the same: the promotion of human welfare.

This book provides valuable practical guidance for those seeking a career in the sciences. Dr. Easton examines the various fields of science, describing educational opportunities, explaining jobs and job requirements, and advising prospective scientists how to succeed in their chosen career paths. Additional sources of information include a bibliography and an appendix listing agencies offering financial aid information.

Because of the nature of their work, scientists will never become obsolete or unnecessary. With each new discovery and achievement comes a whole new set of problems to confront and frontiers to explore. Many exciting challenges and rewards await those who will amaze the generations to come.

Richard C. Atkinson
President
American Association for the
Advancement of Science

PREFACE

"Career development" people think of life in terms of careers. Often, they divide life into five stages:

1. *Growth*. Until about age 14, children develop their understanding of the meaning and purpose of work, try new experiences, and develop their self-image.

2. *Exploration*. Between the ages of 14 and 24, people realize that they need to choose a career. They look at their interests and abilities, consider how they may tie into various occupations, choose a direction for their future, and gain appropriate education, training, and experience.

3. *Establishment*. Between the mid-20s and middle age, people develop their professional competence with further education, training, and experience. They develop occupational status, and they advance.

4. *Maintenance*. Once they have established their professional niche, people devote their efforts to preserving their skills through practice and on-the-job training. They also begin to plan for eventual retirement.

5. *Decline*. After about age 65, people reduce their commitment to work. They adjust the demands of work to their own fading energies. Gradually or suddenly, they shift their attention from their work to themselves.

This scheme was first developed by Donald E. Super in the 1950s. It is still current, for Charles C. Healy uses it to organize his 1982 book, *Career Development: Counseling through the Life Stages*. I mention it because, although I am not going to talk about scientific careers in terms of the five stages, one stage does define the readers of this book. Only "explorers" will be interested in anything with a title like *Careers in Science*. The exceptions will be "establishment" and "maintenance" career counselors, whose job is to help the explorers explore.

However, explorers need not all be under the age of 24. Careers rarely follow any rigid pattern. People do—and should—continue to grow throughout their lives. Many never stop exploring. Some, as soon as they are established in one career, miss the challenge of the early stages. They grow bored or stale, and they begin to look for fresh alternatives. They shift from business to science to law to politics. They may never reach the maintenance stage at all.

Personally, I admire such job-hopping jackrabbits. They sometimes seem to have a keenness and a vitality that others lack. Perhaps they have more interests and competencies. Or perhaps they lack the consuming, absorbing interests that bind others to single careers.

Certainly, any one person begins life with a host of potential careers before him or her. Interests and abilities then determine the amount and nature of the education he or she seeks—a high school diploma, an associate of arts (AA) or science (AS) degree, a bachelor of arts (BA) or science (BS) degree, a master's (MA or MS) degree, or a doctorate (PhD, DA, DSc, MD, or DO). Each level of education leads to certain careers, but not to others without a return to school. That is, a brand-new BS graduate in biochemistry can be a technician but not a university professor. The professorship requires a doctorate, but the BS technician can always go back to school to gain first a master's degree and then the PhD.

Career options need not, of course, be defined only in terms of degrees. I think of a friend who, over 20 years ago, earned his doctorate in health physics and became a researcher with the National Institutes of Health. A few years ago, he enrolled in an administrative training program. He is pursuing a new career option, leaving research for administration. He may eventually become a campus dean or a research and development (R&D) manager.

I think also of researchers who have become teachers (and vice versa), or editors, or writers, or entrepreneurs. In each case, the individual has grown and broadened. However, the individual has also pursued preexisting interests. Never does a scientist become a businessperson unless he or she has cared about product development, management, or sales in the past. Each step in a person's career has its roots in the person and in previous steps.

Each step in a career opens up further steps. On the other hand, each step also closes off some of the early wealth of options. For instance, after 20 years as a biologist, it is difficult—if not impossible—to go back to school and become a geologist, a nuclear physicist, or a mathematician. The shift requires too much time, and the intellectual sponge that once was the college student has usually lost too much of its absorptive capacity.

It is thus wise to make *your* choice carefully at the beginning. Gain all the education you have patience, time, and money for, and gain it in a field that matches your interests and abilities as closely as possible. Do you need help? That is the function of this book. Its topic is the career options available in the sciences. It will discuss the difference between a "job" and a "career." It will say what science is and what kinds of people are scientists. It will present a few statistics on the supply of and demand for scientists. It will try to help you choose a field of science, describe the educational requirements, and present the possibilities in the life, earth, physical, and space sciences and in engineering and mathematics. Finally, it will tell you a little about how to find a job in your chosen field.

Once you have completed this book, you should have a good idea of which fields of science you are most likely to find satisfying and rewarding for years to come. You should know what kinds of jobs in those fields you might fill, where they might lead you, and what education and experience you must gain to qualify for them. You should also know what personal and financial rewards to expect.

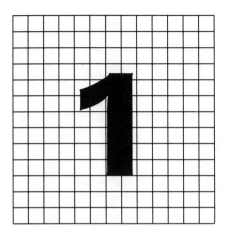

CAREERS AND SCIENCE

Let us begin our discussion of careers in science with a few definitions. What is a "job"? What is a "career"? What is "science"? What is a "scientist"?

"Science" and "scientists" we can define in terms of the scientific method, and we will do just that in a little while. First, however, we must consider more basic matters. Look at Table 1, a "career development glossary" published by the U.S. Office of Education in 1976. With thoroughly academic formality, it defines 15 terms related to work and working, dividing them into three clusters of terms related to time and effort, to content, and to structure. We can take the time and effort cluster for granted, for everyone must expend time and energy in gaining a living; the terms in this cluster contribute little to our purpose here. We can also ignore the structure cluster, for these terms too allow us to draw no useful distinctions.

JOBS VERSUS CAREERS

The content cluster, however, is useful. It tells us that a "job" is a set of tasks or performances by which a person earns the pay necessary to buy food, shelter, clothes, and other goods in our society. A "job" is defined in terms of the effort that goes into it, the results it produces, or the setting in which it is performed. The individuality of the person who does the job is irrelevant.

On the other hand, the person who fills a "career" is essential to the definition of "career." A career is "the sequence of major positions occupied by a person throughout...life." It includes the roles of student, trainee, employee, retiree, family member, citizen, and hobbyist. "Careers exist only as people pursue them; they are person-centered."

Table 1   A career development glossary

Time and effort

Work	The systematic pursuit of an objective valued by oneself (even if only for survival) and desired by others; directed and consecutive, it requires the expenditure of effort. It may be compensated (paid work) or uncompensated (volunteer work or an avocation). The objective may be intrinsic enjoyment of the work itself, the structure given to life by the work role, the economic support which work makes possible, or the type of leisure which it facilitates.
Labor	Productive work for survival or support, requiring physical or mental effort.
Employment	Time spent in paid work or in indirectly paid work such as homemaking.
Leisure	Time free of required paid or unpaid work, in rest, play, or avocations.
Play	Activity which is primarily recreational and relaxing; engaged in for its own sake, it may be unsystematic or systematic, without objective or with an objective which is of temporary and personal consequence; it may involve the expenditure of effort, but that effort is voluntary and easily avoided by the player.

Content

Task	A performance required at work or in play.
Position	A group of tasks to be performed by one person; in industry, performed for pay. Positions exist whether vacant or occupied; they are task- and outcome-, not person-, defined.
Role	A set of behaviors associated with a position. The *role concepts* of persons occupying positions may be so called; those of persons surrounding the position, *role expectations.*
Job	A group of similar, paid positions requiring some similar attributes in a single organization. Jobs are task-, outcome-, and organization-centered.
Occupation	A group of similar jobs found in various organizations. Occupations are task-, economy-, and society-oriented.
Vocation	An occupation with commitment, distinguished primarily by its psychological as contrasted with its economic meaning: ego-involving, meaningful to the individual as an activity, not solely for its productive, distributive, or service outcome and its economic rewards, although these too are valued. Vocations are task-, outcome-, and person-centered.
Avocation	An activity pursued systematically and consecutively for its own sake with an objective other than monetary gain, although it may incidentally result in gain. Avocations are task-, outcome-, and person-centered.
Career	The sequence of major positions occupied by a person throughout his preoccupational, occupational, and postoccupational life; includes work-related roles such as those of student, employee, and pensioner, together with complementary avocational, familial, and civic roles. Careers exist only as people pursue them; they are person-centered.

Structure

Organization	A specific institution, company, or other independent or autonomous entity producing or distributing goods and services.
Industry	A branch of an art or trade which employs people to produce or distribute goods or to provide services; a group of similar organizations.

Source: D. E. Super, *Career Education and the Meanings of Work*, Monographs on Career Education. (Washington, D.C.: U.S. Office of Education, 1976.)

A "job" is a means. It earns the price of survival, of necessities and luxuries. A "career" is intimately involved with one's image of one's self. It is something more than a means. It is an end, a goal, even an ideal.

To this we can add something from the common wisdom. What is a "career man" or a "career woman"? He or she is not just putting in time to earn a paycheck. He or she is pursuing a role or place in society. He or she has a sense of mission, of dedication to more than mere personal or even family survival. He or she has a calling, a "vocation," which brings us back again to Table 1.

Any career begins in school. In fact, it begins before the "careerist" has a chance to make a choice. Elementary school and junior high school build basic skills and interests. High school exposes students to various broad fields such as chemistry, biology, physics, and history. It permits a choice of tracks—college prep, vocational, or business—and it leads to the first major career decisions. Will the new high school graduate get a job immediately? Or will he or she go on to college? Which college will he or she go to?

College often seems more of a starting point for a career than high school, for it is in college that students first meet the fields in which they might actually work. They take courses in organic chemistry and biochemistry, genetics and microbiology, astronomy, calculus, and more. They focus on areas that mesh with their interests and abilities. They gain specific knowledge essential to work in a field. They find problems, questions, and issues to which they can dedicate their lives. They set their sights on future status and role, and they decide whether they need still more education to reach their goals.

Eventually, during or after their schooling, most students become workers. They take a first job, a first "career position" in their field. Later, they decide to pursue further training, to accept or reject responsibility, to shift from teaching to research or business or writing, or even from one field to another. Their career develops as they go from decision to decision and from position to position. In general, the sequence steps from studenthood to an entry-level position of little reward, power, responsibility, or freedom, to later positions of more reward, power, responsibility, and freedom. Careers in science may peak with a deanship on campus, a department chairmanship, a college or university presidency, a senior administrative post with the government, or even the presidency of a private corporation. At less rarefied levels, many scientific careers peak with a rank of full professor or senior researcher. Many more never get that far, and still more of the thousands who work in the fields of science are neither teachers nor researchers. Instead, they are technicians of various sorts, sellers of technical equipment, textbook editors, and so on, and they climb their own hierarchies, perhaps ending as chiefs of labs, heads of sales departments, and editors in chief.

A great many careers are available in science. The variety is awesome, and to the young person peeking tentatively through the entry door, it

Figure 1 The scientific method

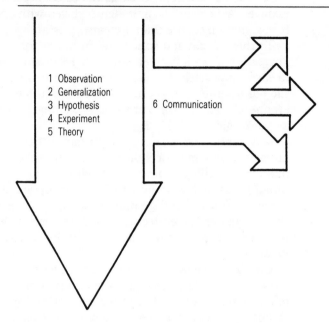

1 Observation
2 Generalization
3 Hypothesis
4 Experiment
5 Theory

6 Communication

may be more than a little frightening. Yet all the careers of science do have one thing in common: science.

WHAT IS SCIENCE?

Science is system. It is the word, drawn from the Latin for "to know," that we use for knowledge we have collected and interpreted in a certain systematic way. We also use the word for the process of collection and interpretation, so that a "scientist" is one who "does science."

We do not use the word "science," as we use "biology" or "physics," to delimit a certain, restricted portion of the study of the world. Absolutely everything does or can fall into the realm of science. (The study of illusory flying saucers, angels, "psychic" spoon-benders, and ghosts, all sometimes called "beyond science," belongs to psychology.)

The system of science is the scientific method (see Figure 1). This method begins with the *observation* of unexplained facts. As the observer studies the observations, he or she sees interrelationships and patterns. The observer *generalizes* a pattern to cover unobserved facts, and devises a tentative explanation of the pattern, a *hypothesis*. The observer then tests this hypothesis on new observations with a planned *experiment*. If the experiment fails to confirm the hypothesis, the observer must formulate a new hypothesis and conduct another experiment. If that experiment does confirm the hypothesis, then the hypothesis becomes part of the observer's stock of knowledge. Thorough, repeated confirmation, along with success in helping to explain new observations, promotes a hypothesis to the status of theory, principle, law, or even fact.

One essential part of the scientific method is *caution*. Researchers go to great lengths to avoid the many kinds of error and bias that can contaminate experiments. They conduct control experiments to be sure that the results they see are real and not unforeseen effects of their experimental setups, and they analyze their results with statistics.

Another crucial part of the scientific method is *communication*. Observation, generalization, hypothesis, and experiment are all useless if they are kept private. A result is not a result—it has no validity, no credibility—if others cannot obtain it too, and they cannot seek it unless they know where and how to look. Thus the scientific worker must publish scientific reports that explain observations, generalizations, hypotheses, and experiments in enough detail for others to repeat the work. Even technicians, spending day after day on standardized tests of water quality or blood sugar levels, must record what they do and observe.

Science is thus firmly based on the notion of repeatability. It has little room for the unique, and for those who keep their methods or findings secret, and even less room for those occasional individuals who invent fraudulent, false observations and experimental results.

Because this demand for repeatability means that every step of a scientist's work must be checkable, science possesses an accountability that other areas may lack. Anyone who contemplates a career in science must thus have a sense of responsibility and duty, a dedication to truth, accuracy, and completeness that supersedes all other loyalties. People with scientific training should find it difficult or impossible to conceal facts to protect their employer's financial or political interests. (They should even find it difficult to protect their own interests in this way.) Unfortunately, employers often have other ideas, and too many scientists have lost their jobs because of their respect for truth.

The scientific method can thus present the scientist with a painful dilemma. So too can other high ideals. If it comforts you, take the pain as a measure of the ideal's worth. If that doesn't help, remember that the world is far from perfect, that no ideal is shared by everyone, and that we must each live up to ourselves as best we can. Many of us manage to find relatively comfortable levels of compromise with our ideals.

SCIENCE AND SURVIVAL

The dedication of science is not to truth alone. The knowledge obtained by the scientific method has many valuable uses. It eases labor with new machines, processes, and materials. It aids health with medications and treatments. It improves the food supply. It finds new sources of energy and raw materials. It reveals and identifies ecological crises such as acid rain, carbon dioxide-induced climate change, and chlorofluorocarbon-caused damage to the stratospheric ozone layer, resulting in dying forests, rising sea levels, and increasing risk of skin cancer; it tells us what to do to end or adapt to these problems. It contributes to our understanding of how people act in groups, hence, how best to lead and govern.

A job serves the jobholder's individual survival. A career in science does that too, but it also serves the survival of the human species. Success in such a career can thus provide immense personal satisfaction. No scientist has ever truly saved the world or the human species from destruction, but many who pursue careers in science have as a result of their labors saved or improved lives, fed the hungry, or warmed the cold. They have identified hazards, and they have found answers. They have made discoveries that spawned industries and employed thousands or millions. They defend us all against the forces of extinction, and their dedication is that of the soldier in love with the battle. Often, they say they are the most blessed of human beings because they are paid for doing what they would do as a hobby if they had to.

WHO ARE THE SCIENTISTS?

The people who follow careers in science are dedicated to truth and human survival. They are also dedicated to the search for knowledge. They live to wrest new facts from nature's grasp and to find new ways to use facts already known. They seek the new in basic research; they use the old in applied research and in the myriad nonresearch jobs of the technicians and engineers. Many also spread the word to students and the lay public by teaching and writing. Very few seek wealth, for they are motivated from within, although applied researchers may come up with new products, drugs, devices, or production methods that pay off handsomely indeed. Occasionally, even basic researchers can find wealth, as in the case of the pioneers of recombinant DNA. Here, the finding of "restriction" enzymes that can cut and splice DNA strands at specific points made it immediately possible, for instance, to transplant genes from one organism to another and to grow human proteins in bacteria. Many of the basic researchers who first discovered how to do this are now involved with successful genetic engineering firms.

THE SCIENTIST'S CHARACTER

Scientists seek knowledge, truth, and human survival, using the scientific method. Potential scientists need the ability to work and think methodically. They must also share several other very particular character traits, for scientists in general are persistent, curious, creative, precise, intelligent, objective, honest, and enthusiastic.

Persistence

Persistence is a matter of never giving up. Scientists seek answers to novel questions, and they try again and again and again when attempted answers don't work out.

A classic example of persistence is the German scientist Paul Ehrlich, who tried 605 different drugs as cures for syphilis before he found the famed "606." Better drugs now exist, but Ehrlich did begin the use of chemotherapy for disease. Today, the development of a new drug may require the screening of thousands of candidates.

Curiosity

Curiosity is a very basic characteristic of the scientific personality. It is essential to basic and applied researchers, but also to the teachers who must encourage it in students; they teach best when they are models of the trait.

What is curiosity? It is the ability to be forever asking questions, and then seeking the answers. The process of asking and answering need not be complicated, as one graduate student's experience shows. He was studying motor reflexes. One of these reflexes appears when cats mate, for the male always (or nearly always) bites the female in the back of the neck. In response, the female assumes an appropriate posture that facilitates the mating. The graduate student asked: Is this reflex necessary to the act? Would blocking it prevent mating, and perhaps offer a method of contraception for house cats, one cheaper than spaying and reversible to boot? He answered: A cardboard shield constructed to cover the back of the female's neck did in fact prevent mating.

This willingness to try out new ideas is the aspect of curiosity that is essential to science. It is the essence of experiment.

Creativity

Many people think that creativity is just for poets, novelists, sculptors, and other artists. But it is also essential for research scientists and teachers. Researchers need it to devise new hypotheses and the experiments with which to test them. Both researchers and teachers must be creative in the ways they express their results and knowledge if they are to communicate effectively with their peers, their students, and the general public.

Precision

Many scientists require a steady, precise hand for manipulating tiny objects, as in dissecting fruit flies or single cells or in repairing electronic equipment. All scientists need a precise mind for noting fine distinctions and avoiding subtle errors. Both mind and hand can be trained, and that is one aim of every college science lab.

Intelligence

Any scientist will find mental alertness, quickness, and agility useful in reaching the top, but genius is not absolutely necessary. Few people can or should set their sights on the Nobel Prize for their career objective. All should be able to reason abstractly and concretely, to solve problems and comprehend new facts, and to trade old notions for new. Some intelligence is essential, but flexibility may be more important than IQ.

Objectivity and honesty

We have already noted that scientists must have a high regard for truth. That is, they must be honest. In addition, and in the service of honesty, they must be objective. They cannot let enchantment with their ideas, or laziness, or haste, keep them from checking their hypotheses with experiments. They cannot hide from critics in the holy cloak of science, believing that because they are scientists, they have a monopoly on truth—or that because they are scientists, whatever they say *is* the truth.

Objectivity requires the strength not to deceive the self. Konrad Lorenz once said it meant discarding a pet hypothesis every day before breakfast. Louis Flexner said, "Although I have great confidence in the observations,...the interpretations...badly need further work to test them."

The truly objective, honest scientist rarely comes out decisively on only one side of an issue. Quizzed before Congress, the scientist states an opinion, but then adds, "On the other hand..." For this reason, our representatives in Washington have more than once wished for a one-armed scientist.

True objectivity is rare, and many nonscientists find it disturbing and even threatening. So do some scientists, who fall short of their own ideals. It is often said, with some justice, that a truly new idea gains acceptance only with the deaths of the older members of the field who refuse to accept it.

Other traits

Honesty, persistence, objectivity, curiosity, precision, creativity, and intelligence are all necessary traits of scientists. Other traits are necessary in particular fields. Any scientist must have a liking, an enthusiasm, for his or her own field. A biologist must care about the animals, plants, and people on which he or she experiments and treat them humanely (only in studies of stress do stressed—pained—organisms yield fully trustworthy data). Outdoor specialists such as wildlife biologists, archaeologists, anthropologists, and geologists need stamina, strength, and outdoor experience. Others may require physical courage, tolerance for heat and cold, or the ability to fly a spacecraft or work in isolation or in crowds. Most specialties call for the ability to work well as part of a team.

SUPPLY AND DEMAND FOR SCIENTISTS AND ENGINEERS

According to the National Science Foundation, in 1984 there were 2,214,100 engineers and 1,781,400 scientists employed in science and engi-

Table 2 Employment of scientists and engineers, 1984

	1984	Percent increase since 1976
Scientists and engineers, total	3,995,500	71
Engineers, total	2,214,100	61
Scientists, total	1,781,400	86
Physical scientists	254,100	35
Chemists	168,600	27
Physicists/astronomers	61,200	38
Other physical scientists	24,300	106
Mathematical scientists	100,400	107
Mathematicians	83,900	93
Statisticians	16,500	217
Computer specialists	436,800	267
Environmental scientists	98,100	79
Earth scientists	82,300	77
Oceanographers	3,200	−27
Atmospheric scientists	12,600	232
Life scientists	353,300	65
Biological scientists	236,600	70
Agricultural scientists	88,700	118
Medical scientists	27,900	−16
Psychologists	209,500	86
Social scientists	329,200	48
Economists	125,600	101
Sociologists/anthropologists	77,700	129
Other social scientists	125,900	0

Source: *Women and Minorities in Science and Engineering,* National Science Foundation Special Report NSF 86-301 (Washington, DC: U.S. Government Printing Office, 1986).

neering jobs (see Table 2). These figures were up about two-thirds since 1976, but they still did not include everyone with a scientific education. Many scientists and engineers work in sales, management, and administration and as writers and editors. Many more seem to lack the status to be included. Thus Table 2 says that 27,900 "medical scientists" were employed in 1984, but there were also over 5.5 million men and women in health-related occupations, including 151,000 dentists, 1,406,000 registered nurses, and 1.2 million nursing aides. It certainly seems reasonable to say that health personnel enjoy careers in science.

The demand for scientists and engineers has been increasing steadily and impressively for decades. The two-thirds overall increase between 1976 and 1984 incorporates truly large gains—over 100 percent—for statisticians, atmospheric scientists, agricultural scientists, and economists. Only two categories—oceanographers and medical scientists—record a decline over the period, while just one, "other" social scientists, shows no change at all (this stasis conceals a decline between 1976 and 1982 and a recovery since then).

That the growth of employment in so many fields of science was so great in the late 1970s and early 1980s indicates a strong demand by society for scientists. This demand seems even stronger when we look at the unemployment statistics, for the unemployment rate for scientists is much lower than that for the labor force as a whole. It rarely rises much above 1 percent, although women may experience unemployment rates of 4 to 6 percent in some fields, and scientists with bachelor's and master's degrees experience somewhat higher unemployment rates than those with doctorates. Demand also looks good when we examine the percentage of recent graduates with jobs in the fields they trained for. In 1980, 58 percent of male and 37 percent of female 1978 and 1979 bachelor's science and engineering graduates held science or engineering jobs. Among master's graduates, the percentages were 85 for men and 67 for women.

Will the demand for scientists remain strong? In the spring of 1988, the U.S. Department of Labor's Bureau of Labor Statistics estimated the prospects for various occupations through the year 2000. Among the occupations expected to show the largest growth in numbers of jobs between 1986 and 2000 (see Table 3) were registered nurses; nursing aides, orderlies, and attendants; computer programmers; computer systems analysts; licensed practical nurses; and electrical and electronics engineers. Among those occupations projected to grow the most rapidly (see Table 4) were medical assistants; physical therapists; physical and corrective therapy assistants and aides; data-processing equipment repairers; homemaker-home health aides; podiatrists; computer programmers and systems analysts; radiologic technologists and technicians; dental hygienists and assistants; physician assistants; operations research analysts; occupational therapists; and optometrists. By contrast to the way scientific and technical occupations dominate these two lists, only statistical clerks and certain equipment operators are to be found on the BLS's list of those occupations expected to *decline* most rapidly between 1986 and 2000.

What's the story for women and minorities? Table 5 shows the percentages of women, blacks, and Hispanics employed in various scientific and technical occupations in 1985, according to the U.S. Department of Labor. It is worth noting that women account for 44.4 percent of all American workers, blacks for 9.9 percent, and Hispanics for 6.6 percent. In most scientific and technical areas, the participation rates for these three groups are significantly less. Women exceed their total workforce participation slightly in the social sciences and dramatically in the health areas. Blacks exceed their total workforce rates only in the areas of health services (aides and orderlies) and technicians (including dental hygienists and licensed practical nurses).

Table 3 Occupations with the largest job growth, 1986–2000 (Numbers in thousands)

Occupation	Employment		Change in employment, 1986-2000		Percent of projected job growth, 1986-2000
	1986	Projected, 2000	Number	Percent	
Salespersons, retail	3,579	4,780	1,201	33.5	5.6
Waiters and waitresses	1,702	2,454	752	44.2	3.5
Registered nurses	1,406	2,018	612	43.6	2.9
Janitors and cleaners	2,676	3,280	604	22.6	2.8
General managers and top executives	2,383	2,965	582	24.2	2.7
Cashiers	2,165	2,740	575	26.5	2.7
Truckdrivers	2,211	2,736	525	23.8	2.5
General office clerks	2,361	2,824	462	19.6	2.2
Food counter and related workers	1,500	1,949	449	29.9	2.1
Nursing aides, orderlies, and attendants	1,224	1,658	433	35.4	2.0
Secretaries	3,234	3,658	424	13.1	2.0
Guards	794	1,177	383	48.3	1.8
Accountants and auditors	945	1,322	376	39.8	1.8
Computer programmers	479	813	335	69.9	1.6
Food preparation workers	949	1,273	324	34.2	1.5
Teachers, kindergarten and elementary	1,527	1,826	299	19.6	1.4
Receptionists and information clerks	682	964	282	41.4	1.3
Computer systems analysts	331	582	251	75.6	1.2
Cooks, restaurant	520	759	240	46.2	1.1
Licensed practical nurses	631	869	238	37.7	1.1
Gardeners and groundskeepers	767	1,005	238	31.1	1.1
Maintenance repairers	1,039	1,270	232	22.3	1.1
Stock clerks	1,087	1,312	225	20.7	1.0
First-line clerical supervisors and managers	956	1,161	205	21.4	1.0
Dining room and cafeteria attendants	433	631	197	45.6	.9
Electrical and electronics engineers	401	592	192	47.8	.9
Lawyers	527	718	191	36.3	.9

Source: R. E. Kutscher, "An overview of the year 2000," *Occupational Outlook Quarterly,* Spring 1988, pp. 3–9

Overall, the figures for women and minorities indicate considerable improvement in employment patterns over the last few decades, thanks to concerted efforts to bring these people onto educational tracks that lead to scientific careers, and to overcome the numerous institutional and social barriers that have long restricted women and minorities to service and low-level jobs. Unfortunately, equal opportunity efforts still

Table 4 Fastest growing occupations, 1986–2000 (Numbers in thousands)

Occupation	Employment		Change in employment, 1986-2000		Percent of projected job growth, 1986-2000
	1986	Projected, 2000	Number	Percent	
Legal assistants	61	125	64	103.7	0.3
Medical assistants	132	251	119	90.4	.6
Physical therapists	61	115	53	87.5	.2
Physical and corrective therapy assistants and aides	36	65	29	81.6	.1
Data processing equipment repairers	69	125	56	80.4	.3
Homemaker-home health aides	138	249	111	80.1	.5
Podiatrists	13	23	10	77.2	0
Computer systems analysts	331	582	251	75.6	1.2
Medical record technicians	40	70	30	75.0	.1
Employment interviewers	75	129	54	71.2	.3
Computer programmers	479	813	335	69.9	1.6
Radiologic technologists and technicians	115	190	75	64.7	.3
Dental hygienists	87	141	54	62.6	.3
Dental assistants	155	244	88	57.0	.4
Physician assistants	26	41	15	56.7	.1
Operations research analysts	38	59	21	54.1	.1
Occupational therapists	29	45	15	52.2	.1
Peripheral electronic data processing equipment operators	46	70	24	50.8	.1
Data entry keyers, composing	29	43	15	50.8	.1
Optometrists	37	55	18	49.2	.1

Source: R. E. Kutscher, "An overview of the year 2000," *Occupational Outlook Quarterly,* Spring 1988, pp. 3–9.

have a long way to go. Women still consistently earn less than men in equivalent positions, and then there is that disparity between specific occupation and total workforce participation rates. This disparity is in large part self-perpetuating, for it means that there are few women and minority role models to convince young people that they too can attain positions in science and engineering. At the same time, the lack of women and minority members in most scientific and technical fields makes it very easy for guidance counselors, parents, and young people to think that those fields are inappropriate or unwelcoming for young women, blacks, Hispanics, and others. The truth, of course, is quite otherwise. Women and minority members have just as much potential as white males to be physicists, physicians, astronomers, engineers—whatever kinds of scientists they want to be.

Table 5 Women and minorities in the scientific workforce, 1985 (Numbers in thousands)

Occupation	Total employed	% Women	% Black	%Hispanic
Total, all fields	109,597	44.4	9.9	6.6
Engineers	1,749	6.0	3.7	2.5
Farming, forestry, fishing	3,444	15.9	6.5	10.5
Health care	2,026	85.3	7.0	2.8
Health services	1,823	89.9	25.1	5.7
Managers, medicine & health	127	62.2	8.1	2.7
Math & computer scientists	631	36.2	7.2	2.5
Natural scientists	384	22.5	2.5	3.2
Physicians & dentists	728	15.0	3.3	3.2
Soc. scientists & urban planners	312	46.0	5.5	2.8
Teachers, college & university	639	36.0	4.0	3.2
Technicians, engineering	937	17.7	6.3	5.3
Technicians, health	1,124	84.1	12.4	3.7
Technicians, science	208	27.9	7.0	4.2

Source: *Employment and Earnings,* Bureau of Labor Statistics, January 1987

Most scientists and engineers are employed by business and industry (see Table 6) in research and development, production, environmental monitoring, mineral exploration, and other activities. The greatest recent growth has been in computer specialties, mathematical sciences, atmospheric sciences, agriculture, and sociology. Future growth, as the new biological technology firms continue to grow, should be strong in the biological and medical sciences.

Table 6 Employment of scientists and engineers by sector, 1984 (000s)

	Business/industry	Education	Federal government
Scientists and engineers, total	2,512	537	307
Engineers, total	1,672	82	167
Scientists, total	840	416	127
Physical	139	61	25
Math	39	46	9
Computer	330	30	29
Environmental	48	16	15
Life	108	131	39
Psychological	47	76	5
Social	130	95	19

Source: *Women and Minorities in Science and Engineering,* National Science Foundation Special Report NSF 86–301 (Washington, DC: U.S. Government Printing Office, 1986).

Educational institutions and the federal government employ far fewer scientists and engineers. In the past few years, it looked for awhile as if these sectors were going to decline in importance, for the federal government seemed devoted to restricting money for scientific and technological research and programs on campus and in government labs, except in defense-related areas. However, a little more money is now going to some areas of science as the federal government has come to recognize the crucial role that science and engineering education and research play in strengthening the American economy. On the other hand, additional forces have been working to restrict the growth of the education sector. The population of college-age youth is shrinking as past declines in the birthrate are felt, and the demand for college and university teachers is relatively static.

In 1986, U.S. students earned 987,823 bachelor's degrees in all fields; 318,504 of these degrees were in science and engineering, and in both categories the numbers were well up from their decline in the early 1980s. The numbers in the social sciences (68,632), the life sciences (53,203), and the physical sciences (21,620) remained depressed. Engineering, mathematics, and computer sciences showed strong increases, reflecting heavy demand in these fields.

The number of doctorates attained was much less than the number of bachelor's degrees attained in all fields. For engineering, the explanation lies in the preemptive demand for bachelor's graduates. In other fields, it presumably lies in the further expense and time of doctoral education, the lesser relative attractiveness of careers in academic teaching and research, and the existence of plenty of careers that require only bachelor's or master's degrees. However, where new engineers are virtually shanghaied from their college commencement exercises, other graduates must make up their minds to seek jobs more deliberately.

The strength of the demand for science and engineering graduates is well shown in the statistics on the transition from college to the working world. These statistics have not changed much since 1980, when, of all the bachelor's degrees awarded, 31 percent were in science and engineering. The engineering graduates, however, received 63 percent of all the job offers and 38 percent of the actual jobs. The science and math graduates received 8 percent of the offers and 15 percent of the jobs. Together, science and engineering copped a disproportionate 71 percent of the offers and 53 percent of the jobs. The only other field that came at all close was business, whose new bachelor's graduates collected 25 percent of the offers and 38 percent of the jobs.

It is well worth noting that the doctorate is by no means essential for a career in science. Overall, most working scientists and engineers have only bachelor's degrees (see Table 8). In fact, agricultural scientists, engineers, computer scientists, and environmental scientists most often have no more than a bachelor's. Mathematicians and psychologists most often have master's degrees. Among employed scientists and engineers, only

Table 7 Science and engineering degrees, 1985–86

	Bachelor's	Master's	PhDs
Engineering	76,333	21,057	3,400
Engineering and industrial technology	19,620	602	10
Physics	4,180	1,501	1,010
Geoscience	1,466	719	252
Geology	4,605	1,515	197
Chemistry	10,166	1,754	1,908
Mathematics	16,306	3,159	742
Computer science	41,889	8,010	344
Agriculture/natural resources	11,264	2,977	258
Life sciences	38,524	5,013	3,358
Health sciences	50,887	15,579	1,188

Source: B. M. Vetter and E. L. Babco, *Professional Women and Minorities,* 7th ed. (Washington, DC: Commission on Professionals in Science and Technology, 1987).

medical scientists and physicists as a group have more doctorates than bachelor's or master's degrees.

We will look at pay scales later in this book, but we might note here the starting pay for various fields. According to the College Placement Council, a 1985 business bachelor's graduate could expect to start at $1,636 per month, and a master's graduate could expect about $2,500. Life science bachelor's graduates could start at anywhere from $1,400 to $2,200 per month. Chemist bachelor's and master's graduates could expect monthly salaries of $1,900 and $2,200 respectively, with $3,000 for a

Table 8 Highest degree level of scientists and engineers

	Bachelor's	Master's	PhDs
Agricultural scientists	55	22	22
Engineers	57	35	3
Computer scientists	65	28	3
Chemists	48	25	27
Environmental scientists	50	32	18
Social scientists	40	35	25
Physicists	18	35	47
Mathematicians	25	55	20
Biological scientists	42	35	23
Psychologists	20	45	35
Medical scientists	15	28	57

Source: Adapted from B. M. Vetter, *The Technological Marketplace: Supply and Demand for Scientists and Engineers* (Washington, DC: Scientific Manpower Commission, 1985), p. 29. Data from National Science Foundation.

new doctorate. Engineers could expect an added $300–$400 per month. Experience, of course, was worth even more.

We will also look at projections for job openings later in this book, as we consider specific careers in the various fields. For now, we must be content with the observation that in most fields of science, the number of openings projected into the 1990s is less than the number of degrees that will be awarded. There is thus some contradiction—supply is higher than demand, but unemployment is low, most science and engineering graduates find work in their fields, and pay is high. The explanation may be that women drop out of the labor market to raise families—their share of science and engineering bachelor's degrees increased by about 50 percent and their share of doctorates by about 150 percent in the 1970s—and that many graduates, both men and women, shift into other fields, even into other science fields, such as the health professions, so they do not show up in the "science and engineering" statistics. High school science teachers are also lost to the statistics.

Whatever the precise explanation, it seems abundantly clear that careers in science and engineering offer ample security and pay, and hence ensure personal and family survival. Because they also serve the cause of human survival on Earth—and perhaps eventually off this planet—they also offer a sense of mission, a dedication that makes life worth living. And, of course, science holds the most fascinating, absorbing, and challenging of topics as well. It is not for everyone, but for those whom it fits, it holds immense personal—and often financial—satisfaction.

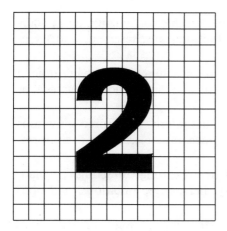

CHOOSING A FIELD OF SCIENCE

It seems reasonable to think that anyone reading a book called *Careers in Science* must already have chosen a life in science. That is, *you* must already find the thought of probing the unknown faces of nature fascinating. You must believe you have the intelligence, creativity, objectivity, curiosity, and persistence to be a scientist of some kind. Perhaps you want to contribute to the survival of humanity in what many think is the most valuable way, by anticipating and solving the problems that arise from life on a small planet.

Many people who choose science—or even one field of science—early in life pursue education to the limits of their ability, patience, and funds. Then they take whatever job they can find in the field they have studied most. That first job leads to others and becomes a career. Yet that career is haphazard. It is far, far better to gather all available information at an early stage. Make an informed choice, and plan. Begin by learning what interests, abilities, and personalities match up with which fields of science. Learn what amount of education is necessary for the career that seems to fit best. Learn where to go for that education and how to fund it.

That knowledge is the fruit you can expect to reap from this book. Let's begin by looking at John Holland's work on personality types and their relevance to career selection.

HOLLAND'S PERSONALITY TYPES

According to Holland (1966), people can be characterized in terms of six different personality types. These are:

1. *Realistic* (R)—interested in mechanical and physical activities; a tool-user; "strong" and "masculine," not socially skilled or sensitive.

2. *Investigative* (I)—interested in thinking, organizing, and under- standing; analytical, intellectual, curious, reserved, and scien- tific, not persuasive or social.

3. *Social* (S)—interested in helping, teaching, and serving others; gregarious, friendly, cooperative, and tactful, not mechanical or technical.

4. *Conventional* (C)—interested in orderly, structured situations with clear guidelines; precise, accurate, clerical, and conform- ing.

5. *Enterprising* (E)—interested in organizing, directing, persuad- ing, and exercising authority; persuasive, ambitious, and opti- mistic; a leader.

6. *Artistic* (A)—interested in performing in sports or arts; emo- tional, aesthetic, autonomous, unconventional, impulsive, and imaginative.

It is hard to think of any person whose personality does not fit this scheme, although almost no one is a pure realistic, investigative, social, conventional, enterprising, or artistic type. People's personalities tend to be predominantly of one type, with admixtures of the others.

The same is true of jobs and careers. Scientists in general must be strongly investigative, but the best scientists often seem to be artistic as well. Social scientists and teachers are also social. The heads of laborato- ries and academic departments and other managers are also enterpris- ing. Engineers are investigative and realistic; mathematicians, investigative and conventional (and perhaps artistic); technicians, realis- tic and conventional.

Holland (1977) has devised a test, the *Self-Directed Search* (SDS), that anyone looking for a career can use by himself or herself. The SDS con- sists of an SDS inventory booklet with which one can generate numerical measures of one's own personality in terms of Holland's six types. That is, a user of the SDS might find that the realistic component of his or her personality measures R = 40, while the other components come in at I = 32, S = 18, C = 30, E = 3, and A = 15. The top three measures then become a summary code, here RIC.

The SDS also includes an *Occupations Finder* that lists 500 occupa- tions by three-letter codes, each code corresponding to a summary code. To use the *Finder,* one looks up the occupations listed under one's sum- mary code (RIC) and its permutations (RCI, IRC, ICR, CRI, and CIR). Holland (1977) then suggests that the user double-check his or her self- ratings of the personality by talking to others who know him or her well and by making sure that potential occupations offer appealing lifestyles (do they involve travel? long hours? working with—or away from—other people?) and that he or she has the ability to undergo the necessary train- ing. The user should also check out the occupations themselves by talking to people in them. College students may check out a potential occupation by taking a part-time or summer job in it. A career counselor may also prove helpful.

CHOICE FACTORS

Personality type is only one of many factors that can go into choosing a career. It is clearly important, though, for people tend to choose careers compatible with their personalities, and if they make a wrong choice, or if their personalities change to lessen compatibility, they may well change their careers. It is no rarity for a businessperson to chuck it all in his or her 40s, to move to a rural area, and to become an artist, or for an artist to go into business. Often, such changes come as a result of a "mid-life crisis," when people realize they are not doing what truly fits them best.

Also important are interests, abilities, past exposures, models, and ambitions. All affect career choices, and all play a part when someone who has chosen the broad field of science narrows that choice down to mathematics, engineering, chemistry, biology, and so on. People choose a field of science in which to work—or a theater in which to do battle—after exposure, in high school or college courses or in part-time jobs, to several possibilities. One field proves most interesting, or it promises a more thorough use of one's talents, or it offers more (or less) exposure to people or machines or wildlife. It may be the field of a favorite teacher, relative, or family friend.

People choose their careers within a field according to their ambitions, imagined roles, and capacities for responsibility and education. The careers themselves then develop with changing interests, with further education and training, and with promotions. Remember that a career is a sequence of positions.

THE FIELDS OF SCIENCE

It is possible to split up the broad area of science in several ways. The broadest split is that between *basic* (or "pure") and *applied* science. Basic science, or basic research, investigates the unknown, seeking new knowledge with little or no regard for its potential uses. Basic science often justifies itself with the argument that *all* knowledge, no matter how useless or irrelevant it may seem at first, eventually proves valuable. This argument has certainly proven right before. Work on large numbers has given rise to "unbreakable" codes. Studies of fungi and bacteria have resulted in the discovery of antibiotics. Research on insect communication with pheromones (odorous substances resembling hormones in function) has yielded new methods of pest control. Work on the behavior of electrons in semiconductors gave us the transistor and other electronic devices; it thus made possible the modern personal computer. The argument may well prove right again; the only real problem with it is that it requires the long view, and those to whom basic research must usually be justified are forced by needs for profit or votes to focus on the short term.

Applied research rarely needs justification. It focuses on ways to use the results of previous basic work, or it seeks answers to specific problems. We see it in efforts to decrease the pollutant emissions of automobile engines, develop weapons from lasers, improve crop yields, and find the causes of new diseases. In each case, there is a clear need and a direction in which to look for the answer to that need.

Applied scientists are not only researchers, however. Engineers follow principles of design to build safe structures. They may use new materials or construct devices never seen before, such as rocket engines and satellites, but they are users of a body of established knowledge. So are the technicians who perform the numerous tests on which medicine, environmental monitoring, and industrial quality control depend. So are the mathematicians and statisticians who compute actuarial tables, analyze census figures, and make sense of the nation's economy. So too are computer programmers, mineral prospectors, and weather forecasters. Perhaps the main difference between these people and the applied "researchers" lies in the sizes of the problems they tackle, in the degree of uncertainty they face. Engineers, technicians, and the rest generally know just what methods to use (the methods may even be specified in a "cookbook" or handbook). Applied researchers must often develop the methods they need. They know only what they need the methods for. Basic researchers may not know even that.

The basic versus applied distinction can be quite helpful to people who are trying to decide on a career in science. How much direction do you need? How much uncertainty can you tolerate in your work? Choose accordingly, and then look at another way of splitting up science into topic areas. These are the "fields of science." They are labels for specialties. They distinguish scientists according to the aspects of nature they focus on. Although they fail to convey the ways the fields overlap, and, by drawing lines between topics, build walls between specialties that require special effort to surmount, they are in fact useful both to the young person looking for a career and to the administrator trying to make a multifield institution such as a university function smoothly.

The helping sciences

All sciences are "helping sciences," for all help our kind survive. However, some are more particularly or directly helpful than others—they help individuals, and they help very much in the short term, in minutes, hours, days, at most a lifetime. The helping sciences include human and veterinary medicine, the allied health professions, psychiatry, clinical psychology, and social work. They treat, ease, cure, and prevent physical and mental illness. They deal also with the poor, the retarded, the handicapped, and the elderly, who may not suffer from illness but do still need helping hands.

The social sciences

Like the helping sciences, the social sciences deal mostly with people. They approach them in groups, though, and they take a larger, more long-term view. These sciences include sociology, cultural anthropology, political science, economics, and social psychology. Their aim is to explain how people behave en masse, in small groups and large, to explicate culture and politics, war and peace, even crime and morality.

The life sciences

The life sciences deal with the phenomena of life. They are the branches of biology—anatomy, botany, ethology, forestry, genetics, herpetology, immunology, physiology, toxicology, virology, zoology, and many, many more. Some touch on nonbiological fields, such as physics and chemistry, but only as these fields pertain to life. Others overlap with the helping and social sciences, but here as they pertain to animals, singly and in groups, as well as humans; their aim is to build overall schemes that put human behavior in an evolutionary, biological context. Still others, such as pharmacy, relate to medicine, but medicine is merely biology applied to questions of health.

Does life fascinate you? Do you itch to know how it ticks or what makes it tick? Then perhaps you should become a biologist. What kind of biologist? Do you care most for plants, animals, bacteria, or viruses? For reptiles, fish, birds, or mammals? For structure or function? For inheritance? For fossils or agriculture or behavior? Whatever your answer, biology has a branch for you. There are even two for the science fiction fan: space biology deals with the reactions of earthly organisms to the space environment; exobiology is the theory (no real data yet exist) of extraterrestrial life.

The physical sciences

The physical sciences are those that deal with nonliving matter. Chemistry is one, with its chief branches of analytical, physical, organic, and inorganic chemistry and biochemistry. Speaking very broadly, it studies the ways atoms and molecules interact. Its discoveries yield fuels, fertilizers, plastics, pesticides, adhesives, and warnings of the potentially disastrous effects on world climate of carbon dioxide and chlorofluorocarbons. Traditionally dependent on the laboratory and the test tube, it now leans almost as heavily on computer simulation as it strives to understand how catalysts work, to design better catalysts, to design ionic traps and filters, and more.

Physics is another, and it brackets chemistry in its purview. At one extreme, it studies the behavior of matter in bulk, the flow of fluids and the movements of objects affected by changing forces, dealing with friction and inertia. At the other, it studies atoms and their constituent parts. Its results yield nuclear reactors and bombs, novel electronic devices, high-temperature superconductors, photovoltaic devices for solar power, turbines that withstand the strains of high winds, strong water

THE RIGHT JOB

Many young people are interested in science, but they have little idea of just what they would like to spend their lives doing in science. One way to narrow down the options is to look at the job requirements (such as initiative, leadership, or stamina), the work environment (hazardous, outdoors, or confined), and the occupational characteristics (pay, entry requirements, or opportunities) of various scientific and technical jobs and consider how they match the budding scientist's, engineer's, or technician's personality, interests, and educational ambitions.

Figure 2 lists over 70 jobs categorized by 17 job requirements, work environment features, and occupational characteristics, which include the following:

Job Requirements
1. Leadership/persuasion—organizing others, supervising, directing.
2. Helping/instructing others—treating, teaching, listening, counseling.
3. Problem-solving/creativity—designing, inventing, drawing, writing, and developing ideas or programs.
4. Initiative—determining what needs to be done and completing jobs without close supervision.
5. Working as part of a team—interacting cooperatively toward shared goals.
6. Frequent public contact—dealing with the public on a regular basis.
7. Manual dexterity—operating tools, testing, drafting, etc.
8. Physical stamina—enduring long-term stress and strain (e.g., heavy lifting).

Work Environment
9. Hazardous—working with infectious materials or where accidents are common (such jobs require careful attention to safety precautions).
10. Outdoors—spending a major portion of the work day outdoors, usually without regard to the weather.
11. Confined—staying in a specific place for most of the work day.

Occupational Characteristics
12. Geographically concentrated—50 percent or more of the jobs in five or fewer states.
13. Part-time—often requiring less than 35 hours per week.
14. Earnings—L = lowest (10 percent or less); M = middle (11–19 percent); H = highest (20 percent or more) (based on 1985 averages).
15. Employment growth—L = lowest; M = middle; H = highest (based on projected growth to 1995).
16. Number of new jobs, 1984–95—this number is usually much *less* than the number of job *openings* created by the need to replace workers who change occupations or leave the labor force.
17. Entry requirements—L = requires a high school education or less, basics can often be learned on the job; M = requires post-high school training such as apprenticeship or junior college, or many months or years of experience, to be fully qualified; H = usually requires four or more years of college.

A chemist needs more than a college education, must be able to solve problems and show initiative, and can expect moderate job prospects and high earnings. Engineers also need to be able to solve problems and show initiative, but they typically work in teams. In some specialties, the work is geographically concentrated. In most specialties, the job and earnings prospects are quite high.

Figure 2 provides an equivalent amount of information for many other jobs, and it makes abundantly clear that there is something in science for almost everyone who cares to look.

Figure 2 Matching Yourself with the World of Work

	Job requirements								Work environment			Occupational characteristics				
	1. Leadership/persuasion	2. Helping/instructing others	3. Problem-solving/creativity	4. Initiative	5. Work as part of a team	6. Frequent public contact	7. Manual dexterity	8. Physical stamina	9. Hazardous	10. Outdoors	11. Confined	12. Geographically concentrated	13. Part-time	14. Earnings	15. Employment growth	16. Number of new jobs, 1984–95 (in thousands)	17. Entry requirements
Engineers, Surveyors, and Architects																	
Architects			●	●	●	●	●							H	H	25	H
Surveyors	●			●			●	●		●				M	M	6	M
Engineers																	
Aerospace engineers			●	●	●							●		H	H	14	H
Chemical engineers			●	●	●									H	H	13	H
Civil engineers			●	●	●									H	H	46	H
Electrical and electronics engineers			●	●	●									H	H	206	H
Industrial engineers			●	●	●									H	H	37	H
Mechanical engineers			●	●	●									H	H	81	H
Metallurgical, ceramics, and materials engineers			●	●	●									H	H	4	H
Mining engineers			●	●	●									H	L	2	H
Nuclear engineers			●	●	●									H	L	1	H
Petroleum engineers			●	●	●							●		H	M	4	H
Scientists and Mathematicians																	
Computer and Mathematical Occupations																	
Accountants and auditors		●	●		●	●						●		H	H	307	H
Actuaries			●	●								●	●	H	H	4	H
Computer systems analysts	●	●	●	●	●							●		H	H	212	H
Mathematicians			●	●										H	M	4	H
Statisticians			●	●										H	M	4	H
Physical Scientists			●	●										H	M		H
Chemists			●	●										H	L	9	H
Geologists and geophysicists			●	●	●					●		●		H	M	7	H
Meteorologists			●	●	●									H	M	1	H
Physicists and astronomers			●	●										H	L	2	H
Life Scientists																	
Agricultural scientists			●	●										1	M	3	H

continued

Figure 2 Matching Yourself with the World of Work

	Job requirements						Manual dexterity (7)	Physical stamina (8)	Hazardous (9)	Work environment		Geographically concentrated (12)	Part-time (13)	Occupational characteristics			
	1. Leadership/persuasion	2. Helping/instructing others	3. Problem-solving/creativity	4. Initiative	5. Work as part of a team	6. Frequent public contact	7. Manual dexterity	8. Physical stamina	9. Hazardous	10. Outdoors	11. Confined	12. Geographically concentrated	13. Part-time	14. Earnings	15. Employment growth	16. Number of new jobs, 1984–95 (in thousands)	17. Entry requirements
Scientists and Mathematicians (continued)																	
Life Scientists (continued)																	
Biological scientists		●	●											H	M	10	H
Foresters and conservation scientists		●	●	●				●	●	●				H	L	2	H
Social Scientists and Urban Planners																	
Economists		●	●											H	M	7	H
Psychologists		●	●	●		●								H	H	21	H
Sociologists		●	●			●								H	L	2	H
Urban and regional planners	●		●	●	●	●								H	L	2	H
Social workers	●	●	●	●	●	●								M	H	75	H
Agricultural, Forestry, and Fishing Occupations																	
Farm operators and managers	●	●	●	●	●			●	●		●			M	L	–62	L
Health Diagnosing and Treating Practitioners																	
Chiropractors	●	●	●	●	●	●	●							H	H	9	H
Dentists	●	●	●	●	●	●	●							H	H	39	H
Optometrists	●	●	●	●	●	●	●							H	H	8	H
Physicians	●	●	●	●	●	●	●					●		H	H	109	H
Podiatrists	●	●	●	●	●	●	●							H	H	4	H
Veterinarians	●	●	●	●	●	●	●	●	●					H	H	9	H
Registered Nurses, Pharmacists, Dietitians, Therapists, and Physician Assistants																	
Dietitians and nutritionists	●	●	●	●	●	●								M	H	12	H
Occupational therapists	●	●	●	●	●	●	●	●						1	H	8	H
Pharmacists	●	●	●	●	●	●						●		H	L	15	H
Physical therapists	●	●	●	●	●	●	●	●						M	H	25	H
Physician assistants	●	●	●	●	●	●	●							M	H	10	M
Recreational therapists	●	●	●	●	●	●	●	●		●				M	H	4	M
Registered nurses	●	●	●	●	●	●	●	●	●				●	M	H	452	M

continued

Figure 2 Matching Yourself with the World of Work

	Job requirements									Work environment				Occupational characteristics			
	1. Leadership/persuasion	2. Helping/instructing others	3. Problem-solving/creativity	4. Initiative	5. Work as part of a team	6. Frequent public contact	7. Manual dexterity	8. Physical stamina	9. Hazardous	10. Outdoors	11. Confined	12. Geographically concentrated	13. Part-time	14. Earnings	15. Employment growth	16. Number of new jobs 1984–95 (in thousands)	17. Entry requirements
Registered Nurses, Pharmacists, Dietitians, Therapists, and Physician Assistants (continued)																	
Respiratory therapists	●	●	●	●	●	●	●							M	H	11	L
Speech pathologists and audiologists	●	●	●	●	●	●								M	M	8	H
Health Technologists and Technicians																	
Clinical laboratory technologists and technicians		●		●		●						●		L	L	18	3
Dental hygienists		●		●	●	●	●						●	L	H	22	M
Dental laboratory technicians							●					●		L	M	10	M
Dispensing opticians	●	●	●		●	●	●							M	H	10	M
Electrocardiograph technicians	●	●			●	●	●							1	M	3	M
Electroencephalographic technologists and technicians	●	●			●	●	●							1	H	1	M
Emergency medical technicians	●	●	●	●	●	●	●	●	●	●				L	L	3	M
Licensed practical nurses		●			●	●	●	●	●				●	L	M	106	M
Medical record technicians				●								●		L	H	10	M
Radiologic technologists		●			●	●	●		●					L	H	27	M
Surgical technicians		●			●	●	●							L	M	5	M
Health Service Occupations																	
Dental assistants		●			●	●	●	●					●	L	H	48	L
Medical assistants		●			●	●	●		●					L	H	79	L
Nursing aides		●			●	●	●	●	●				●	L	H	348	L
Psychiatric aides		●			●	●		●	●					L	L	5	L
Educational and Administrative Occupations																	
College and university faculty	●	●	●	●	●	●		●					●	H	L	-77	H
Health services managers	●	●	●	●	●	●								H	H	147	H
Inspectors and compliance officers, except construction		●	●	●		●			●					H	L	10	M
Statistical clerks				●								●		L	L	-12	L

continued

Figure 2 Matching Yourself with the World of Work

	1. Leadership/persuasion	2. Helping/instructing others	3. Problem-solving/creativity	4. Initiative	5. Work as part of a team	6. Frequent public contact	7. Manual dexterity	8. Physical stamina	9. Hazardous	10. Outdoors	11. Confined	12. Geographically concentrated	13. Part-time	14. Earnings	15. Employment growth	16. Number of new jobs, 1984–95 (in thousands)	17. Entry requirements
Educational and Administrative Occupations (continued)																	
Computer and peripheral equipment operators		•		•		•					•			L	H	143	M
Technologists and Technicians Except Health																	
Engineering and Science Technicians																	
Drafters			•		•						•			M	M	39	M
Electrical and electronics technicians		•		•		•								M	H	202	M
Engineering technicians		•		•		•								M	H	90	M
Science technicians		•		•		•								M	M	40	M
Computer programmers		•		•								•		H	H	245	H
Electrical and Electronic Equipment Repairers																	
Commercial and electronic equipment repairers		•	•		•	•								L	M	8	M
Communications equipment mechanics		•	•		•	•								M	L	3	M
Computer service technicians		•	•		•	•								M	H	28	M
Electronic home entertainment equipment repairers		•	•		•	•		•					•	M	M	7	M

[1] Estimates not available.
[2] Less than 500.
[3] Vary, depending on job.

Source: adapted from Melvin Fountain, ''Matching yourself with the world of work,'' *Occupational Outlook Quarterly,* Fall 1986, pp. 3–12.

currents, and flight. Its results also contribute on a very fundamental level to chemistry, biology, astronomy, and geology.

Caught between chemistry and physics is materials science. Within its purview are the substances we use to make things. It pays great attention to surfaces, strengths, and durabilities, and it contributes to engineering.

The earth sciences

The earth sciences study the Earth. Geologists consider the planet's structure and history, as revealed in its rocks. Geochemists focus on the chemical processes responsible for rock and ore body formation. Geophysicists look at the larger processes that have folded rock layers and moved the plates of the Earth's crust about. Their payoff is understanding of the human species' only home, as well as better knowledge of how and where to find oil, gas, metal, and other raw materials essential to civilization.

The earth sciences also include oceanography, which focuses on the oceans, their bottoms and waters, sediments and currents; and meteorology, which examines the atmosphere. Both fields strive to understand and predict winds and storms and rains, to forecast changes in heat and nutrient flow that affect fisheries. Both feed into the field of climatology (as do the space and other earth sciences), where fluctuations in ocean temperature, solar output, jet stream paths, volcanic dust clouds, and more are integrated to understand and predict the planet's climate.

The space sciences

Astronomy is the first space science that comes to mind. Its subject is the classification, movements, and natures of the stars and planets. It is the science of telescopes, optical and radio, visual and—these days—electronic, on the ground and in orbit. There is also astrophysics, which strives at great distances to grasp the processes that generate and operate dust clouds, stars, and planets, and cosmology, whose aim is to know how all things began.

There are more. With the excursions of the Viking and Mariner and Pioneer probes was born the field of planetology, in essence the "earth sciences" of alien worlds, based on photographs, radar, and limited samples. There is astronautics, the science and art of building and guiding spacecraft. There are space biology and exobiology (see above) and space medicine.

At the moment, the space sciences do not employ a great many people, but our species stands poised on the verge of a great leap outward. We are just now capable of moving into space, of building colonies in orbit and setting others on hostile, alien worlds, and there are signs that we may do these things—or some of them—within our own lifetimes. The future may well need a great many space scientists, perhaps especially in astronautics and space biology and medicine, in the still unformed fields of orbital engineering and low-gravity agriculture, perhaps even in exobiology and in extraterrestrial anthropology, psychology, and sociology. Eventually, when we undertake to make Mars or Venus more like Earth, we will need planetary engineers to "terraform" the planet into livability.

Engineering

Engineers are humanity's builders and makers. They design and oversee the construction of cars, trains, ships, aircraft, and spacecraft, of farm equipment, highways, buildings, factories, and mines. They develop artificial organs, ceramics, metal alloys, and mechanisms. They are in great demand, essential, and well paid.

Mathematics and computer science

Computer science blends mathematics and electronic engineering. It adds cognitive psychology in its studies of artificial intelligence, and it rests firmly on logic and philosophy in its programming aspect. Like engineering, it is highly applied, in great demand, and well paid. It is also glamorous, for computers are coming to dominate civilized life as both tools and games, and they are already shaping the lifestyles of the future.

Mathematics, either pure or applied, is the systematic manipulation of numbers, magnitudes, and symbols. It is arithmetic, algebra, geometry, and calculus, measurement and statistics, modeling and projection. It is necessary in every field of science and business, but it is far less glamorous than computer science. Pure mathematics is largely an academic pursuit, studying number theory, abstract algebras, and the like. Applied mathematics is very practical, finding niches in the insurance industry (actuaries), government (statisticians), and science and industry in general (measurers, calculators, modelers, and theoreticians). Its value to coding means that jobs exist in military, security, and intelligence agencies. Its value as a form of logic and its close relation to the computer sciences have led to the field of systems analysis, essential to modern decision making.

HAVE YOU CHOSEN?

Have you chosen your field of science yet? Basic or applied? The helping or social sciences? Biology or chemistry? Physics or the earth sciences? A future in space or engineering? Mathematics, perhaps? Or computers?

You may indeed already have a strong sense of where your future lies. However, you should not yet make a final choice. That must hinge on a deeper acquaintance with specific careers, which you will begin to gain later in this book. It may also depend on your capacity and inclination for education, for different careers call for different degrees, and the highest levels may require years of schooling and training.

Chapter 3 will outline the educational requirements and expenses of careers in science. It will not attempt to prescribe specific schools for specific fields, but it will point to some of the many available sources of financial aid.

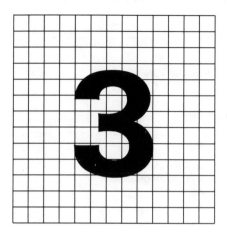

GETTING THERE

How can you become a scientist? The process is neither quick nor simple. It is the same as the answer to any other question of becoming: You work to acquire the skills and knowledge appropriate to your chosen career. And it takes years.

We tend to think of scientists as people who have displayed the research talent, scholarly creativity, and patience required to earn doctoral degrees. This is true enough for teachers on college and university campuses and for researchers on campus and in industry and government laboratories. But it is hardly a complete picture. A great many people who can call themselves scientific workers do not have doctorates. Lab technicians and many health workers may have no more than a two-year (associate) or four-year (bachelor's) college degree. High school science teachers and many engineers may have a bachelor's or master's degree. Teachers at two-year colleges may have only a master's degree or the non-research-oriented doctor of arts (DA).

Some scientific workers actually have no degrees at all. They have acquired their skills and knowledge through on-the-job experience, perhaps in the military, and they are just as well qualified as their degreed fellows. They may actually be more qualified; often, during the time others have spent in a classroom, they have been developing a deep and intimate practical acquaintance with their subject. They can be engineers, naturalists, archaeologists, fossil-hunting paleontologists, geologists, foresters, and more.

It is thus one of the sadder facts of life that many employers insist on degrees as proof of qualifications. They also ask for experience, for that does demonstrate fitness for a job, but they too rarely settle for experience alone. Therefore, your best path to your chosen career will combine degree and experience. The experience may come in summer or part-

Figure 3 Educational pathways

WORK	EDUCATION	LEVEL
Transitional, dead-end jobs	High school	0
Lab technicians, paramedics, nurses, allied health workers, etc.	Two-year college (community college and vocational school)	1
High school teachers, lab technicians, allied health workers, engineers, foresters, etc.	Four-year college	2
High school and two-year and four-year college teachers, research associates, foresters, engineers, etc.	Graduate school master's degree	3
College and university teachers, industry and government researchers and managers, physicians, dentists, etc.	Graduate school doctorate (PhD, DA, DS) Professional schools (medical, dental, veterinary, law)	4

Note that in pursuing a career, more than one graduate degree can be acquired at levels 3 and 4.

time work, in assisting a professor's research, or in a few years' work between high school and college or between college and graduate school. The experience will help not only in landing a job but also in providing a better grip on more academic classroom learning.

Figure 3 shows some of the many possible educational pathways. One can go directly from high school to a doctorate, though many people pause to work awhile between the stages of their educations. The stages we can call "levels," and we can use the levels to characterize various careers. Level 1 careers, such as technician, need at least two years of college. Level 2 careers need four years. Level 3 careers need a master's degree. Level 4 careers call for at least a doctorate.

The arrows in the figure stake out most of the possible pathways. A high school graduate can enter the job market directly or go on for a two- or four-year degree. A college graduate can get a job or another degree. One can pause between any two stages of one's education to work, or one can go all the way to a doctorate before starting the working phase of a career.

Note that the arrows suggest that people can obtain more than one master's degree or doctorate. A medical researcher may need both a PhD and an MD. A patent lawyer may need both a law degree and a master's or doctorate in science or engineering. A manager may need to add an MBA to his or her science or engineering degree. Rare individuals may acquire several master's or doctorates; they occasionally seem to have chosen careers as perpetual students.

LEVEL 0: HIGH SCHOOL PREPARATION

Those who are considering a career in science, no matter how much education they hope or plan to acquire, should begin their preparations in high school. They should take every science course available—biology, chemistry, physics, geography, and more if possible. These courses will provide a first real taste of science and a first exposure to the various fields of science. They will provide a first chance to discover whether science really appeals and a first, light sampling of the available specialties.

In addition, the would-be scientist should take all the mathematics courses available, up to and beyond calculus, for mathematics is often called the language of science. A course or two in computers and computer programming will also prove very useful, since there is virtually no branch of modern science that does not use computers extensively.

A good knowledge of the English language is also essential, for the scientist must be able to communicate clearly, concisely, and precisely. Scientists must be able to say what they mean without confusion and in as few words as possible. Unfortunately, many scientists fail on this count. Too much scientific prose is wordy, murky, jargon-laden, and confusing. It slows reading and learning, aggravates journal editors, and worsens the writer's chances of communicating and of being promoted.

Bear in mind that everyone appreciates a good speaker and writer. All students—not just would-be scientists—should thus take plenty of English courses and practice their composition. They should read all they can, pay attention to how writers write, and try to match what they read in their own efforts. As they become better writers, they will be pleased to find how much easier writing becomes.

Foreign languages are very useful. Most graduate schools once required a reading knowledge of two foreign languages. Most now ask for no more than one; if a second *is* required, it may be a computer programming language such as COBOL, BASIC, or LISP. The one human language should be a language that the student will find it useful to be able to read in his or her field, one in which reports he or she wishes to read are published. Once this meant German, since most non-English-language research was once done by Germans. Now it means German, French, Spanish, Russian, or Japanese. Before long, Chinese may belong on the list. German, French, and Spanish are offered in many high schools. Russian and Japanese should be, for they are now the more useful to many scientists.

Fortunately, a great deal of foreign research is published in English, and most of the scientists who meet at international scientific meetings at least speak English as a second language. However, the ability to read and even speak some language other than English is invaluable for more than simply satisfying academic requirements. Its professional benefit is speedier, more effective communication. Many people believe it is also valuable for the way it opens another culture—its music, literature, and history—to the person who speaks or reads its tongue. Whatever their reason, students should begin acquiring other languages early in their education. Later, they will need the time languages demand for study in their specialties.

High school students should *not* neglect their other courses, for scientists are as much a part of the world as anyone else and must know as much about it. Still, if they do concentrate on their professional preparation, they will also be well prepared to switch to other fields, even to a nonscience such as history or politics. Preparation for science, because it is so broad and inclusive and because it inculcates the habits of a logical, orderly mind, is preparation for almost anything. Those who have trouble making up their minds in high school may do well to bear this in mind and to remember that few college students have chosen their careers before their junior year. Some are still undecided in—or after—graduate school.

LEVEL 1: THE TWO-YEAR EDUCATION

High school graduates who want to pursue their education nevertheless may not go directly to a four-year college or university. They may not be able to afford the high tuition. They may not qualify for various financial aid programs. They may not wish to take out a loan to cover the costs of four years of full-time schooling.

Perhaps they are just plain sick of school, or uncertain of their career direction. They want to work for a year or two, to gather experience, sample possibilities, and save money for later schooling. When they do return to school, they may do so tentatively, attending classes part-time or in the evening. They may very well look for a less expensive school or seek education that prepares them quickly and specifically for better jobs. Already, they may have no patience for the smorgasbord approach that helps so many college students find their careers. They may want education more tailored to the interests they develop as they work.

Professional schools fill this need for college graduates. There are also numerous four-year technical schools. But what is there for students with lower immediate aspirations and slimmer purses?

The extension (or "continuing education") courses offered by state universities have traditionally met these students' needs. Now there are also many junior or community colleges that offer two-year associate of arts (AA) or science (AS) degrees, often with a very vocational emphasis. There are two-year programs for lab technicians in biology and other sciences, and for allied health workers. There are also two-year technical and vocational institutes, trade schools, and formal and informal apprenticeship programs.

The great virtue of these programs is that they offer a slower, less intensive, and less expensive approach to higher education. They also prepare their students to transfer to a four-year school to obtain a bachelor's degree in two more years, while also offering a natural stopping point after the AA or AS. They do *not* offer a lower quality education, although two-year schools, like four-year schools, do vary in quality. They *do* offer a briefer, and hence less extensive, education. For many, they are a first step. For some, they are enough, for they do prepare one adequately for many careers.

The greatest drawback to a two-year education may be its lack of breadth. The four-year liberal arts education, which cultivates not job skills but the abilities to think and live well in the world, impresses many as coming much closer to producing a well-rounded, even an ideal, human being. On the other hand, the "school of hard knocks" can have a very similar effect.

LEVEL 2: THE FOUR-YEAR EDUCATION

The four-year schools are colleges and universities. The educations they offer vary greatly in quality but less in kind. These schools generally follow one of two approaches to educating their students. The first is the liberal arts approach. It encourages students to take a wide variety of courses, both to broaden their minds and to expose them to many possible career directions. In their second and third year of college, students choose a "major" field, in which they then concentrate on their studies. This approach is common in small colleges.

The second, professional approach appears more often in technical schools and institutes and in large universities. In the latter, students may enroll at the start in a school of forestry or engineering or business and choose a major within that narrow field. In a school of arts and sciences, they may also find a more liberal education, with majors in English, biology, or anthropology. Often, students begin broadly in arts and sciences and later move into a field-oriented school.

The professional approach often gives students specific job skills. It equips them to step into a job immediately. The liberal arts approach transmits a body of more general knowledge. Often, its avowed aim is to teach habits of thought and study. It thus equips students less for jobs than for further education, perhaps in graduate school or in the form of on-the-job training.

Each field of science has its own body of knowledge, and the college student begins to acquire that knowledge with an introductory survey course. Later courses cover specialties within the field in greater depth. For instance, a college freshman who wants to major in chemistry will take "Freshman Chem" for an overview of the field of chemistry and its basic principles. Later, he or she will take "Organic Chemistry," "Biochemistry," and "Physical Chemistry." Larger schools may also offer courses in "Quantum Chemistry," "Catalysis," and "Spectroscopy."

In all the sciences (except mathematics and some social sciences), most courses are accompanied by a laboratory. Here, students learn the techniques of the field and specialty they are studying. They may even learn techniques that amount to job skills, but many schools do not have laboratory equipment nearly as up-to-date as the working labs of industry and government. Students often learn the skills of a past generation of scientists and must depend on their knowledge of methods and principles to help them catch on quickly once they are out of school. They usually succeed, but many scientific educators are deeply concerned with this disparity between education and practice. They yearn for industry, government, and foundation funding to buy modern equipment. Fortunately, the government has recently been reaffirming the value of science and education and expressing its own concern over outdated laboratory equipment. Funding improvements may be just around the corner. If they are not, and in the meantime, students may have to depend on part-time and summer jobs to bring their technical skills up to current standards, or rush to catch up once they have their first career positions.

Science students should take all the courses and labs within their major field for which they have the time. But they should also do more. They should take English courses to boost their communication skills, both written and oral. They should learn the use of computers. They must study math and statistics, a requirement that cannot be too strongly emphasized. Statistics is essential in the designing of experiments and for the analysis of data in every field. Math is equally essential to understanding and to building explanatory models or theories, and while all the sciences use calculus and differential equations, some use abstract algebras, tensor calculus, fiber bundles, and other mathematical esoterica.

Science students should also take science courses outside their field. Biologists and astronomers invariably need at least a good grounding in chemistry and physics. Engineers and geologists need biology, chemistry, and physics. Chemists need physics. Physicists need chemistry. All can benefit from taking at least the survey courses in each of the other fields.

There are limits, however. In a small school, students can hope to take every available course in their major field and the survey courses for every other science represented on campus. At a large university, they may not have the time to take even half the courses in their major, and they may have to pick and choose very carefully to find the survey courses most pertinent to their major. Too, the large university may demand more specialization at the bachelor's level—the student will major in zoology or biochemistry or solid-state physics instead of biology, chemistry, or physics. Nevertheless, the student should gain as broad a scientific education as possible. It will not be wasted. It may even prove invaluable, for the greatest discoveries are often made by people who can combine the concepts or data of two or more fields.

Many students approach college with their field already in mind, and they look for a school with a top reputation in that field. If that school does not accept them, they feel like failures before they have even begun their careers. Yet it is not only the biggest schools with the most varied offerings and the most glittering reputations that are worth attending. Small, relatively unknown schools can offer excellent preparation for a career in science, and many outstanding scientists have come from small colleges best known only within a single state or region. The small liberal arts schools have, for instance, graduated a number of top biologists all out of proportion to their collective size. The best way to judge a school may be, if it offers the necessary basic courses, to ask whether its graduates have been able to enroll in top graduate schools or to win choice positions in industry and government.

Every student, in every school, will benefit tremendously from actual experience in his or her specialty. This experience can take the form of serving as a teaching assistant in lab courses, a job often open to undergraduate seniors. It can mean helping a faculty member in research. It can mean part-time or summer jobs off campus, working in industry, research labs, museums, parks, or zoos. Such experience provides a taste of the future and a basis for changing one's mind. It may also introduce a student to research interests that will prove absorbing throughout a long career. In addition, it can help pay the costs of a college education.

LEVEL 3: THE MASTER'S DEGREE

Less than a third of all science and engineering bachelor's graduates go on to earn a master's degree in their original field or a related field. Those who do spend one or two more years in school, taking more specialized courses than they could find in college and learning skills more closely related to what they will need on the job. They do not usually get involved in their own original research. The thesis often required for the master's degree depends more on the library than on the laboratory. Its function is to demonstrate command of a body of knowledge.

Many people set a master's degree as their goal. The degree is the one they need for the career they have in mind. They have no interest in original research. They do not, at this point in their lives, plan to become researchers or professors. And their needs are met by most graduate schools.

However, some schools—or some departments within many schools—do not offer the master's degree as an end in itself. They see it as a way station, a certificate that says one has made a certain amount of progress toward a doctorate. They may offer it as a consolation prize for students who decide not to complete the push for a doctorate, either because they have run out of patience or because they have found the limits of their ability.

LEVEL 4: THE DOCTORATE

Depending on the field, 2 to 20 percent of science and engineering bachelor's graduates go on to earn a doctorate. The percentage is lowest in computer science, agriculture, and engineering, where the demand is highest for people in bachelor-level jobs. In computer science and engineering, bachelor's graduates receive pay so high that they have little incentive to stay in school. The percentage of doctorates is highest in physics and chemistry, which employ many researchers (see Table 7).

The doctorate marks the highest level of educational achievement in this country. The first U.S. PhD (doctor of philosophy) program was set up by Yale University in 1860, and the PhD is now *the* degree of the skilled teacher, scholar, and researcher. The requirements for the PhD vary some from school to school and from field to field, but they always include the fact of specialization. It is in graduate school that biologists become ichthyologists and geneticists, physicists specialize in optics and particle theory, chemists focus on catalysts and spectroscopy. In the process, they satisfy foreign language requirements, pass an intensive exam on their knowledge of their specialty (and perhaps collect a way-station master's), select an original research topic, do the research, write a thesis or dissertation presenting the results of that research, and defend the thesis or dissertation orally before a faculty committee. The object of their ordeal—which can last five or more years—is to ensure that all new PhDs know their field and are capable of original contributions to it. Along the way, they may assist in teaching and research, learning the practical skills they will need and helping pay their educational and personal bills.

There are alternatives to the PhD at the doctoral level. The DSc (doctor of science) is an equivalent degree offered by some schools, perhaps in an effort to distinguish scientists from nonscientists. The DA (doctor of arts) is for those who plan to make a career of teaching, with little or no research; it emphasizes preparation for teaching. The MD (doctor of medicine) is for those interested in the healing applications of science, especially of biology. Medical schools offer both classroom learning and clinical experience in a hospital. Other specialized professional schools train veterinarians, dentists, optometrists, and osteopaths; they offer their own degrees.

In the case of medicine, further specialization may follow medical school and the MD. There is some room for specialization within a medical program, but neurologists, proctologists, cardiac surgeons, and other specialists gain many of their unique skills in later internships and residencies, working in hospitals under older experts; their postgraduate training is a combination of seminars and hands-on apprenticeship. Even with no time out for work experience, physicians may thus not be fully trained until their 30s. The youngest physicians are produced by a few schools with special programs; these schools accept highly qualified high school graduates and give them both premedical and medical training in six to seven years.

Students facing four years of college and up to five (or more) years of graduate training often find the prospect a depressingly long grind. Yet every career requires a long apprenticeship, years of training, and skill building. The high school, community college, or college graduate who begins his or her working career immediately, without further academic schooling, must spend those years on the job. The big differences are that the job pays, while school costs, and that on-the-job training produces no paper certification of education or competence.

The long apprenticeship is just as necessary for musicians, writers, artists, businessmen, and politicians as it is for scientists. Doctoral-level scientists emerge from graduate school as young as 26 or 27 or, if they took off a few years for work experience, in their early 30s. They have a degree that documents their abilities. They may even, in their doctoral research, have already made a valuable contribution to the scientific literature, for it is not at all unusual for graduate students to publish their original work. Students thereby act as fully professional research scientists, and they underline the definition of career as including the years in school.

PAYING FOR SCHOOL

The four levels of education beyond high school correspond roughly to four levels of careers. Where a high school graduate cannot become much more than a laboratory gofer ("Go fer this, go fer that"), a stockroom clerk, a veterinary attendant, or a trainee technician, the worker with a two-year degree can be a trained lab technician, an allied health worker, or an engineering aide. The four-year college graduate can be an engineer, forester, medical technician, or high school teacher. A master's degree opens up the field of college teaching, provides entrée to scientific research, and lets one attain higher levels as a technician or engineer. A doctorate lets one join the faculties of major schools, take charge of research, or practice medicine.

Each of these four levels of education and career is attainable. All the beginner needs is interest and intelligence and a willingness to work hard. Patience and determination help. The motivation can be curiosity, ambition, or simple greed, for at each level one's income does go up.

The biggest obstacle may be the expense of education. College tuition can run to many thousands of dollars a year, although state universities may be much less expensive. Room, board, texts, and other expenses may run the student's budget to well over $15,000 a year. Lucky students can tap their families for the funds they need, at least as undergraduates. Less lucky students must find their funds themselves.

Fortunately, it *is* possible to find the necessary money. Part-time and summer jobs help. Some students work full time and take courses as they can afford them. Many employers will pay tuition and allow time off for studies for their employees. Some will pay for a student's education in return for a promise that the student will work for them for a certain number of years after graduation. In cooperative education, the student alternates periods of on-campus schooling with paid on-the-job experience. Internships place advanced undergraduate and graduate students who have already gained a fair amount of competence in their field in part-time professional settings and can involve pay; more often they are for academic credit only.

There are also scholarships and grants available to those who qualify for them. Some are small and some large. Many schools have their own, representing donations intended to help, for instance, "left-handed Congregationalist orphans" (the example is only half facetious). Others come from such outside sources as the Daughters of the American Revolution, churches, foundations, and the National Merit program. College catalogs are useful sources of information. So are the state educational agencies listed in the Appendix. Still others are listed in Figure 4.

There are also loans. Of most interest are those with low interest rates and repayment guaranteed by the government. Guidance counselors and college financial assistance offices have the necessary information. Some loans need no repayment at all if, after graduation, the student works in a specific place for a specific employer for a few years. Medical students may pay their way by agreeing to work in out-of-the-way areas; the money may come from the federal government, a state, or even, occasionally, a town that desperately needs a doctor.

The Student Guide to Federal Financial Aid Programs describes five major student financial aid programs offered by the U.S. Department of Education, along with the necessary application information.

- *Pell Grants* are the most common form of aid, going to about 80 percent of low-income students. The maximum award for the 1987–88 school year was $2,100. As a grant, this money need not be repaid.

Figure 4 Financial aid information

The A's and B's: Your Guide to Academic Scholarships, Victoria A. Fabish (Alexandria, VA: Octameron Associates). Annual.

Annual Register of Grant Support: A Directory of Funding Sources (Wilmette, IL National Register Publishing Co.). Annual.

Directory of Financial Aids for Women, 1985–1986, Gail Ann Schachter (Santa Barbara, CA: Reference Service Press, 1985).

Don't Miss Out: The Ambitious Student's Guide to Scholarships and Loans, Robert and Anna Leider (Alexandria, Va: Octameron Associates). Annual.

Facing the College Cash Crunch, John Mock (Pompano Beach, FL: V.I. Press, 1984).

Financial Aid for Higher Education, Orum Keesler (Dubuque, IA: Wm C. Brown). Biennial.

Higher Education Opportunities for Minorities and Women (Washington, DC: U.S. Department of Education). Annual.

How and Where to Get Scholarships and Financial Aid for College, Robert Leslie Bailey (New York: Arco, 1986).

How to Pay for College or Trade School: A Dollars and Sense Guide, Richard B. Lyttle and and Frank Farrar (New York: Franklin Watts, 1985).

Need a Lift? To Educational Opportunities, Careers, Loans, Scholarships, Employment (Indianapolis, IN: The American Legion Education Program). Annual. Write: American Legion, National Emblem Sales, Box 1050, Indianapolis, IN 46206.

Lovejoy's Guide to Financial Aid, Robert Leider (New York: Monarch Press, 1985).

The Scholarship Book: The Complete Guide to Private Sector Scholarships, Grants and Loans for Undergraduates, Daniel J. Cassidy (Englewood Cliffs, NJ: Prentice-Hall, 1984).

The Student Guide to Federal Financial Aid Programs (Washington, DC: U.S. Department of Education). Annual. To get a copy, call (301) 984-4070 or write to Federal Student Aid Programs, P.O. Box 84, Washington, DC 20044.

To obtain those items published by the federal government, you should check your local library or career guidance office, write to the source (here, the U.S. Department of Education), or phone the Superintendent of Documents, U.S. Government Printing Office, at (202) 783-3238 for price and ordering information.

Source: Adapted from Neale Baxter, "A primer on scholarships for the talented," *Occupational Outlook Quarterly,* Summer 1987, pp. 9–18.

- *Supplemental Educational Opportunity Grants,* administered and distributed by the school, provide up to about $4,000, depending on need.
- The *College Work-Study* program pays students to work (for a limited number of hours) for the school or elsewhere in jobs that serve the public interest.
- *Perkins Loans* (formerly National Direct Student Loans), as loans, must be repaid. They carry low (5 percent) interest rates. In 1987–88, they offered up to $4,500 to students in the first two years of their college education, up to $9,000 to third- and fourth-year students, and $18,000 for graduate or professional study. For first-time borrowers, repayment starts nine months after graduation and may take up to ten years. Repeat borrowers start repayment six months after graduation.

- *Guaranteed Student Loans* (including PLUS loans and Supplemental Loans for Students) are low-interest loans made to students by financial institutions such as banks and are insured (guaranteed) by state and federal agencies. They provide up to $2,625 per year for first- or second-year undergraduates, $4,000 per year for third- and fourth-year students, and $7,500 per year for graduate students. Repayment begins six months after the student graduates or leaves school and may take five to ten years. PLUS loans permit parents to borrow up to $4,000 per year, to a total of $20,000, for each qualifying student dependent. Supplemental Loans for Students allow students to borrow the same amount on top of the Guaranteed Student Loan.

Something to bear in mind is that very few students pay all their college expenses—or even most of them—with loans. Even low-income students (or their families) tend to cover no more than half the bill with loans. The rest is covered by need-based grants, scholarships, work-study programs, and part-time and summer jobs. The way the payment pattern works can be illustrated by a brief look at Colby College, a small, high-quality, liberal arts school in Waterville, Maine. It attracts many students from well-off families, but it is not closed to students with less money. Like a great many schools in this country, it provides vast amounts of financial aid.

In the 1960s, Colby's tuition was about $1,400 per year. By 1987, that figure had risen to $10,430, with room, board, fees, and other expenses (such as books) bringing the total to over $16,000 per student. That total did not include travel.

Colby's financial aid process begins with a "needs analysis" which takes into account the student's family's current income, number of children in college, expenses, and assets, and sets an "expected contribution" of the family toward the student's expenses. Since this figure is often considerably less than the student's expenses, the school then offers student loans, parent loans, and part-time jobs on campus (in the bookstore, dining service, and school offices) by which the student can earn up to $1,300 per year. Colby also administers scholarships and grants, including the federal Pell Grants and Supplemental Educational Opportunity Grants. In addition, in 1986–87, Colby supplied about $3,000,000 in grants from its endowment.

Many people recommend that college freshmen not try both to work and to study. College is a very different place from high school. The student must adjust to a new social and physical environment, to a heavier workload, and to new study habits. While this adjustment is still going on, students should not—if possible—make things harder for themselves by taking on extra work. Unfortunately, this means that college students should have their first year's expenses in hand at the start. This may be difficult, if not impossible, and the situation does not seem likely to improve. Costs do keep going up.

Graduate school is less of a financial problem. Many schools will go to great lengths to help promising students complete their studies. They have teaching and research assistantships, paying both stipend and tuition. They have access to government training grants, industry and foundation money, and other sources, and they use these funds to keep the best students. This means that good students need not worry, but it also means that many graduate school classes are taught by older students. The nominal professors may rarely emerge from their labs, preferring to let their teaching assistants handle what they see as a chore. This needn't be all bad, however. Some researchers are stimulating lecturers, but some are not. Their assistants may actually be much better teachers.

The professional schools are less helpful. There are scholarships, but more often students must borrow the money they need. Financial assistance for medical school (to take one type of professional school as an example) can come from a diverse array of loans and scholarships. Loans can come from banks, the Health Professions Student Loan Program, or the Department of Education's Guaranteed Student Loan Program. Scholarships can come from the schools, the National Science Foundation, the Defense Department's Armed Forces Health Professions Scholarship Program (funds to be repaid by service as a commissioned officer), or the National Health Service Corps Scholarship Program (funds to be repaid by working for at least two years in a "health manpower-shortage area"). Most medical schools discourage part-time work because medical study is so demanding.

Not every student qualifies for scholarships or grants. Loans are much easier to get, even though students may balk at the thought of putting themselves tens of thousands of dollars in hock for years to come. Perhaps it will help if we try to put these loans in perspective. A medical student may owe, say, $100,000 by the time he or she is a practicing physician. This is certainly a forbidding sum, but a young physician can easily make $50,000–60,000 a year; if he or she is a specialist in an urban area, that sum can double or triple. It seems little trouble for the physician to repay the $100,000 in as little as five years. Even counting the interest on the loan, the physician will still have plenty of money left to support a comfortable lifestyle.

A bachelor's, master's, or PhD graduate cannot expect to earn a physician's pay, but then he or she won't need to borrow as much money either. At the same time, the degree will increase the graduate's income enough to make repaying the loan relatively painless. This is especially true in fields such as engineering and computer science.

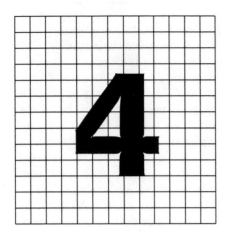

CAREERS IN THE HELPING AND SOCIAL SCIENCES

By far the great majority of science careers are related to health. Physicians, nurses, psychologists, opticians, hospital administrators, medical technicians, and many more add up to some 5.5 million people. The other people-related sciences—the social sciences—employ another 300,000 men and women. All the other sciences combined—the life, earth, space, and physical sciences, engineering, mathematics, and the computer sciences—employ only 3.5 million people.

Most of this book will be devoted to the latter group. The less people-related sciences are, after all, much more what we think of when we think "science," and we are more likely to have them in mind when we think of careers in science. However, careers in health and in social science *are* careers in science. Furthermore, health careers as a group will grow faster than average as the aging of the American population increases the need for health care. In fact, medical assistants, physical therapists, physician assistants, optometrists, and other health occupations dominate the 20 careers with the highest projected growth rates through the year 2000 (see Table 4). Licensed practical nurses, nursing aides, orderlies, and attendants, and registered nurses are among the 27 careers with the highest projected growth in employment over the same period (see Table 3).

Careers in health and social science thus deserve at least a little attention here. Therefore, each of 36 careers in the helping (health-related) sciences and 5 careers in the social sciences has a single section below. The careers are those listed in the U.S. Department of Labor's *Occupational Outlook Handbook*. Their brief descriptions include necessary education, numbers employed, employment outlook, and pay. Most of the data are as of 1986.

Table 9 lists the occupations described in this chapter and summarizes their job prospects through the year 2000 and the educational level they call for (see Chapter 3 for definitions of the levels).

Table 9   Job prospects in the helping and social sciences

Occupation	Percent change in employment, 1986–2000 (NA = Not available)	Educational level
Chiropractor	NA	3
Clinical laboratory technologist/technician	24	1,2
Dental assistant	57	1
Dental hygienist	63	1,2
Dental laboratory technician	39	1
Dentist	30	3,4
Dietitian/nutritionist	34	2
Electrocardiograph technician	16	0,1
Electroencephalograph technician	42	0,1
Emergency medical technician	15	1
Inspector/compliance officer	13	2
Health service manager	56	2,3,4
Licensed practical nurse	38	1
Medical assistant	90	1
Medical record technician	75	0,1
Nuclear medicine technologist	23	1,2
Nursing aide	33	0
Occupational therapist	52	2
Ophthalmic laboratory technician	27	1
Optician, dispensing	46	1
Optometrist	49	3
Pharmacist	24	2,3
Physical therapist	87	2,3,4
Physician	38	4
Physician assistant	57	1
Podiatrist	77	3,4
Psychiatric aide	8	0
Radiologic technologist	65	1,2
Recreational therapist	49	1,2,3
Registered nurse	44	1,2
Rehabilitation counselor	21	3
Respiratory therapist	34	0,1,2
Social worker	33	2,3
Speech pathologist/audiologist	34	3
Surgical technician	33	1
Veterinarian	46	3,4
Economist	34	2,3,4
Psychologist	34	2,3,4
Social scientist	NA	2,3,4
Sociologist	NA	2,3,4
Urban and regional planner	19	3

CAREERS IN THE HELPING SCIENCES

Chiropractor.   Chiropractors believe that many human ills lie in misalignments of the body, especially the spine. They use X-rays to locate the source of trouble, and they treat with manual adjustment, diet, exercise, and other therapies. State certification requires two years of college followed by four years at a chiropractic college. New chiropractors begin at about $20,000 a year; experienced chiropractors average $55,000. There are 32,000 practicing chiropractors in the country, and employment seems likely to grow well through the year 2000, as public acceptance continues to grow.

Clinical laboratory technologist/technician.   The nation's 239,000 clinical (or medical) laboratory technologists and technicians do blood, pathological, immunological, chemical, and other tests in hospital and commercial laboratories. Their work is essential to careful, accurate, thorough diagnosis. Technologists require four years of training; technicians need two. To start, technologists average about $20,000 per year; technicians get about $16,000. Experienced technologists get up to $26,000 and technicians $20,000. The federal government pays its employees in these positions somewhat less. The job outlook is about average.

Dental assistant.   Dental assistants prepare materials, pass instruments, take X-rays, and instruct patients in a dentist's office. They must graduate from a one- or two-year program at a community or junior college, trade school, or technical institute. The 155,000 employed in this job average annual salaries of $11,000–12,000, peaking at about $20,000. The employment outlook through the year 2000 is excellent.

Dental hygienist.   Dental hygienists take X-rays, clean teeth, and instruct patients in proper tooth care. The 87,000 in the field all graduated from accredited dental hygiene schools, most with two-year programs, some with bachelor's or master's programs. The job outlook is good, and the pay runs up to $23,000 per year. However, many jobs in this field are only part-time positions.

Dental laboratory technician.   The dental lab tech makes dentures, crowns, and braces, needing only a high school diploma plus three or four years of on-the-job or apprenticeship training. Some 46,000 people hold this job, making about $19,000 per year. The outlook for this job is excellent.

Dentist.   Dentists clean, repair, and replace teeth; they may also perform surgery on the gums and jaws. The 151,000 practicing dentists have a bachelor's or master's degree plus a two- or three-year dental school degree and average about $60,000 a year. Employment seems likely to grow faster than the average for all occupations through the year 2000, partly because the number of older Americans, who will need a greater amount of dental care, is increasing.

Dietitian/nutritionist. Dietitians and nutritionists provide nutritional counseling, run institutional food services, and educate the public. Numbering 40,000, their salaries average $20,400 a year after obtaining a bachelor's degree and spending 6–12 months as an intern. The job outlook is above average.

Electrocardiograph technician. ECG (or EKG) techs run the equipment that records the electrical activity of the heart for the use of physicians in diagnosing heart disease. There are about 18,000 of them, earning $13,000–25,000 a year. Education can be high school plus either on-the-job training or a one- to two-year academic program. The job outlook is good, with employment expected to grow about as fast as the average for all occupations through the year 2000.

Electroencephalograph technician/technologist. EEG techs operate the equipment that makes brain wave recordings (electroencephalograms) for the use of neurologists in the diagnosis of strokes, tumors, epilepsy, and the like. About 5,900 men and women earn $15,000–20,000 annually in this field. Most learned their skills on the job after graduation from high school. Also available are one- to two-year academic programs. The job outlook is excellent.

Emergency medical technician. EMTs ride ambulances to provide on-the-spot medical aid. Numbering 65,000, they earn $19,000–24,000 a year. Training comes as special programs run by police and fire departments and hospitals and as special courses in medical schools, colleges, and universities. The job outlook is average.

Health service manager. Subject to boards of directors and other governing groups, health service managers manage clinics, hospitals, nursing homes, and other providers of medical care. They oversee budgets, rates, personnel, and planning; raise funds; and handle public relations. There are about 274,000 such managers, many of whom work long hours for pay that runs between $30,000 and $60,000 a year; some earn over $100,000. The education for the job can mean a bachelor's, master's, or doctorate in hospital or health administration or in public health; one can also enter the field with a degree in personnel administration, public administration, or business. Thanks to recent growth in graduate programs in this field, competition for jobs is strong, and the higher degrees are essential for the best-paid positions. The strongest demand may be in group practices, health maintenance organizations, and nursing homes. Employment is expected to grow much faster than average.

Inspector/compliance officer. The 125,000 federal, state, and local health and regulatory inspectors enforce the laws and regulations governing health and safety hazards, trade and employment practices, and immigration. Their duties vary widely, according to whether their spheres are consumer safety, food, agriculture, environmental health, immigration, customs, or occupational safety and health. Federal inspectors need a minimum of a bachelor's degree, or three years of responsible work experience, or a combination of the two, and must pass an exam. They then start at about $15,000 per year; with experience, they move up to $31,000 per year. Nonfederal pay scales are comparable. The job outlook is somewhat below average, thanks to the government's go-slow attitude toward regulation of all types.

Licensed practical nurse. LPNs provide much hospital bedside care, assist physicians and registered nurses, administer medications, instruct patients, make appointments, and take medical histories. They number 631,000, earn annual salaries of $15,600 in hospitals and $15,000 in nursing homes on the average, and are graduates of one-year programs offered at technical, trade, and vocational schools; at community colleges; and in the military. Many schools do not require, but do prefer, a high school diploma for admission. Employment is expected to rise much faster than average through the year 2000.

Medical assistant. Medical (or medical office) assistants serve as receptionists and as recorders of patient data, perform simple laboratory tests, prepare patients and instruments, and instruct patients. Most of the 132,000 in this country earn $10,000–16,000 a year and are high school graduates trained on the job by the physicians who employ them in their offices. In 1986, over 7,000 graduated from one- and two-year medical assistant programs offered by community colleges and vocational schools. The job outlook is excellent.

Medical record technician. Medical record technicians develop and maintain medical information systems. Numbering about 20,000, they transcribe, analyze, code, and file medical data; maintain registries; compile statistics; and abstract records. In small institutions, they run the system. They need a two-year associate degree and make $13,000 to $25,000 a year. Employment should grow much faster than average as the health field and its associated paperwork continue to expand.

Nuclear medicine technologist. Technologists in the field of nuclear medicine carry out diagnosis and treatment of disease using radioactive chemicals. They may also do research, implement safety procedures, and operate diagnostic imaging equipment (also a task of radiologic technologists). In 1986, nuclear medicine technologists held about 9,700 jobs, mostly in hospitals. Training programs last from one to four years and culminate in a certificate or an associate or bachelor's degree. Pay starts at an annual average of about $20,000 and moves up, with experience, to over $25,000. Employment will grow about as fast as the average for all occupations through the year 2000.

Nursing aide.   The nation's 1,224,000 nursing aides help care for the ill, the disabled, and the infirm. They work in hospitals, where they may also be known as orderlies, nursing assistants, or hospital attendants, and in nursing homes, where they may be called geriatric aides. They require no more than a high school diploma, and they average under $11,000 per year. The field will have an ample supply of openings through the year 2000.

Occupational therapist.   Occupational therapists work as part of a medical team to help patients develop independence, develop or regain skills, prepare to return to work, and adjust to disabilities. They require a bachelor's degree (although master's degrees are available), number 29,000, and make about $21,000 a year to start. Experienced therapists average about $26,000 a year. Administrators may make up to $39,000 a year. The job outlook is very good.

Ophthalmic laboratory technician.   Ophthalmic lab techs or optical mechanics make prescription eyeglasses, following the prescription of an ophthalmologist, dispensing optician, or optometrist. The 24,000 in this occupation learned their skills on the job; through formal, three- to four-year apprenticeship programs; or through six-month to two-year programs at community colleges, vocational and technical institutes, or trade schools. Classed as skilled workers, they start at $10,000–15,000 per year. Employment should grow faster than the average for all occupations through the year 2000.

Optician, dispensing.   Dispensing opticians accept eyeglass prescriptions, measure patients to fit eyeglasses, instruct ophthalmic lab techs, and adjust the finished product. Numbering about 50,000, they learn their skills on the job, in two-year programs, and in a few shorter programs. They earn $15,000–20,000 a year; self-employed dispensing opticians can make $30,000 and more. The job outlook is above average.

Optometrist.   Optometrists diagnose eye problems and prescribe lenses and treatment, supply glasses, and fit and adjust glasses. The 37,000 practicing optometrists in this country each hold a four-year doctor of optometry degree from a college of optometry, on top of two or three years of pre-optometric study at a college, university, or community college. (Many students enter colleges of optometry with a bachelor's degree in hand.) New optometry graduates can expect to earn about $30,000 a year; experienced optometrists average about $60,000 a year. The job outlook is very favorable, with employment expected to grow much faster than average through the year 2000.

Pharmacist. Pharmacists dispense drugs prescribed by physicians and dentists, maintain patient drug records, and advise customers on nonprescription medications. Of the 151,000 pharmacists working in 1986, most worked in community pharmacies (drugstores). All had a four-year BS or bachelor of pharmacy degree from a college of pharmacy. Most of these colleges require one or two years of pre-pharmacy education at a college, university, or community college; some accept high school graduates. A few colleges of pharmacy also offer the doctor of pharmacy degree, which requires a total of six or seven years of education after high school. New pharmacists can start at annual salaries of $22,500 (federal minimum) or $26,700 (hospitals). With experience, they can make much more. Employment will grow as fast as the average for all occupations through the year 2000.

Physical therapist. Physical therapists treat patients to restore bodily function, relieve pain, or prevent permanent disability after disabling injury or disease; they work with physicians. They number 61,000 and have bachelor's degrees (master's and doctoral degrees are also available); over a third of their number work in hospitals. They start at about $22,000 per year in hospitals and $18,000 per year with the federal government. The federal average is $26,400 per year.

Physician. Physicians diagnose and treat human illness and advise patients on its prevention. Some also do medical research. The 491,000 active U.S. physicians all have MD (doctor of medicine) or DO (doctor of osteopathy) degrees. MDs, who have graduated from medical schools, have spent at least four years of study to earn a bachelor's and another four to earn the MD. Most have also spent three years in a residency program, where they learned the special skills necessary for a specialty in cardiology, surgery, pathology, neurology, internal medicine, ophthalmology, proctology, dermatology, obstetrics, and so on.

Osteopaths, who emphasize the muscles, bones, ligaments, and nerves of the human body, treating illness with manual manipulation as well as surgery, drugs, and other accepted medical tools, have completed three or four years at an osteopathic college. Osteopathic colleges require at least three years of college for admission, but most of their students have a full bachelor's degree. After graduation, most osteopaths spend a year as an intern. Specialists in pathology, physical medicine and rehabilitation, surgery, proctology, and other fields study intensively for another two to five years.

A new medical graduate, still in his or her residency program, can expect to earn $20,000–24,000 a year. After the residency, income shoots skyward, with the average physician making $106,300 in 1985. The job outlook is very favorable, for the population is growing (albeit slowly) and there is a swelling proportion of elderly people, who demand more medical attention.

Physician assistant.   Physician assistants take medical histories, perform medical exams, order lab tests, make tentative diagnoses, and prescribe treatments, working under the supervision of physicians. The 26,000 in this occupation in 1986 (up from 9,500 in 1980) were graduates of programs, often two years in length, in colleges, universities, medical schools, and community colleges. The requirements for admission to these programs varied from a high school diploma to a bachelor's degree. Pay starts at about $23,400 a year; overall, physician assistants average about $27,500 a year. Employment should continue to grow much faster than the average for all occupations through the year 2000.

Podiatrist.   Podiatrists specialize in problems of the feet. They diagnose the problems and treat them with surgery, drugs, and corrective devices. The 13,000 active podiatrists are graduates of four-year colleges of podiatric medicine, which they entered after at least three years of college. They may also have served a one-year residency. The pay starts low but commonly rises to over $63,000 a year. The job outlook is much better than average.

Psychiatric aide.   The nation's 88,000 psychiatric aides (also known as mental health assistants, psychiatric nursing assistants, and ward attendants) help care for the mentally ill in mental hospitals, halfway houses, community mental health centers, and drug abuse and alcoholism treatment programs. They require no more than a high school diploma, and they average under $11,000 per year. The field will have an ample supply of openings through the year 2000.

Radiologic technologist.   The nation's 115,000 radiologic technologists use X-rays and other imaging techniques to picture and diagnose problems within the human body. They may also use radiation to treat cancers and other illnesses. Subspecialties include radiographers (diagnostic X-rays), radiation therapy technologists (radiation treatment of cancers), and sonographers or ultrasound technologists (they use sonar-like high-frequency sound waves to scan the body's interior). Training programs range in length from one to four years and result in a certificate, an associate degree, or a bachelor's degree; the associate degree is the most common. Salaries start at an annual average above $17,000 and, with experience, exceed $25,000. Radiation therapy technologists earn the most. Employment should grow much faster than the average for all occupations through the year 2000.

Recreational therapist.   Recreational therapists, or therapeutic recreation specialists, number 29,000. Most work in nursing homes and psychiatric and rehabilitation hospitals, where they use leisure activities as treatment for the mentally, physically, and emotionally disabled. They thus resemble occupational therapists. Formal training is required for entry into this field, and there are 170 college and university programs available; 64, most of them offering a bachelor's degree, were accredited in 1986. Associate degrees (enough for many nursing home jobs), master's, and doctor's degrees are also available. Pay varies, with nursing homes offering as little as $11,500 a year; hospital recreational therapists start at an average $19,000 a year. Employment should expand much faster than the average for all occupations through the year 2000.

Registered nurse.   Registered nurses are famous for the quality they contribute to hospital care. They monitor patient progress, administer medications, teach health care, and maintain an atmosphere conducive to recovery. Registered nurses may also work in private homes, schools, community and industrial clinics, and physicians' offices. They may also teach on campus. They numbered 1,406,000 in 1986. Registered nurses have graduated from a two-year associate degree program, a two- to three-year "diploma" program, or a four- to five-year bachelor's degree program. A bachelor's degree is generally essential for supervisory positions. Master's and doctorate programs are also available. Some post-bachelor's programs equip RNs to become nurse practitioners, who have added diagnostic and assessment responsibilities in pediatrics, geriatrics, mental health, midwifery, and medical-surgical nursing. The pay averages about $17,000 a year, with supervisory nurses making over $33,000. The job prospects are excellent due to the current shortage of trained nurses.

Rehabilitation counselor.   Rehabilitation counseling is but one specialty within the field of counseling, which encompasses 123,000 workers. Rehabilitation counselors help people overcome physical, mental, and emotional handicaps by inventorying talents, skills, and interests and encouraging suitable training. They have master's degrees in rehabilitation counseling, counseling and guidance, or counseling psychology, and they average about $30,000 a year. Employment should grow about as fast as the average for all occupations through the year 2000.

Respiratory therapist.   The nation's 56,000 respiratory therapists treat patients with heart and breathing problems. They provide temporary relief to asthma and emphysema victims and emergency care to victims of heart failure, stroke, drowning, shock, poisoning, and head injury. Most therapists gain their training in two-year associate programs; bachelor's degrees are also available. Technicians usually have a certificate from a one-year program. The average annual starting pay for therapists is $17,800, moving up with experience to over $22,000 annually. The job outlook is above average.

Social worker. The nation's 365,000 social workers help people deal with mental, emotional, marital, and economic troubles. They work in welfare agencies, mental health clinics, alcoholism and drug abuse clinics, and elsewhere. Many have only a bachelor's degree in the field. Higher-level positions require a master's. Bachelor's social workers have an average annual starting pay of about $17,000. Master's social workers can start at about $21,000 per year and with experience average upwards of $27,000 per year. The job outlook is better than average, although it is more than usually subject to fluctuations in public policy.

Speech pathologist and audiologist. Speech pathologists and audiologists strive to diagnose and remedy or compensate for defects in speech and hearing. They number 45,000, and their standard credential is a master's degree. They start at $22,500 a year. With experience, they average over $28,000 a year. Employment should increase faster than average until the year 2000.

Surgical technician. In 1986, 37,000 men and women worked as surgical technicians, preparing operating rooms and patients for surgery, passing equipment to surgeons, handling specimens, and working sterilizers, lights, suction machines, and diagnostic equipment. Most community college, hospital, and vocational and technical school training programs last nine months to a year; some last two years. Some surgical technicians are trained on the job. The starting pay runs about $13,600 annually; experienced technicians earn an average of $18,500 annually. The job outlook is better than average.

Veterinarian. Veterinarians are specialists in the prevention, diagnosis, and treatment of animal diseases and injuries. Numbering 37,000 in 1986, they have four-year degrees from colleges of veterinary medicine. Most veterinary students already have a bachelor's degree; all veterinary schools require at least two years of college for admission. Veterinarians employed by the federal government started at annual salaries of $22,500 or $27,200 in 1987 and with experience averaged $41,300. Veterinarians in private practice can earn much more. Employment is expected to grow much faster than average through the year 2000.

CAREERS IN THE SOCIAL SCIENCES

Economist. The nation's 59,000 economists deal with the interactions of labor, raw materials, finance, and finished goods to describe and predict the behavior of the economy as a whole. Many specialize in labor, transportation, marketing, energy, agriculture, or other fields, and advise government, business, unions, and financial institutions. A third of all economists work in colleges and universities. The best jobs go to economists with doctorates, but jobs exist for those with bachelor's and master's degrees as well. With the federal government, bachelor's economists start at about $15,000 per year, master's at about $22,500 per year, and economists with doctorates at about $27,000 per year. Federal economists average over $40,000, as do economics professors on campus. Economists in business enjoy salaries averaging over $50,000 per year. Employment of economists should grow faster than the average for all occupations through the year 2000.

Psychologist.   The nation's psychologists are students of human behavior. Forty percent of them are *clinical psychologists* serving the needs of the mentally and emotionally disturbed. Other specialties include developmental, experimental, personality, comparative, social, physiological, educational, counseling, school, industrial, engineering, and community psychology. Psychologists who choose a life of research and teaching in colleges and universities need a doctorate; so do clinical psychologists in many states. A master's degree may be enough for community college teaching, psychological testing, and other jobs. Doctoral psychologists average over $39,000 per year. A bachelor's degree is worth about $15,000 per year to start. A master's degree with one year of experience is worth about $22,000 per year to start. Employment should increase faster than the average for all occupations through the year 2000.

Social scientist.   Social scientists study human society in all its aspects in order to help us understand how people make decisions, wield power, and respond to change and to the need for change. They include economists, anthropologists, geographers, historians, political scientists, psychologists, sociologists, and urban and regional planners. Altogether, they form a group of 199,000 people, a quarter of whom are self-employed as counselors, consultants, and so on. The rest work for government agencies, research organizations, consulting firms, businesses, health facilities, and so on. Still more work as faculty members for colleges and universities, though their numbers have not been broken out of the total of 754,000 such teachers.

Social scientists as a whole averaged almost $30,000 per year in 1986. Starting pay for bachelor's graduates was about $21,000. Social scientists with doctorates averaged in salary between $37,200 and $46,100. Federal social scientists made somewhat less. Employment of social scientists should expand faster than average through the year 2000, but this growth will be mainly among psychologists and economists. In general, the best job opportunities will exist for those with doctoral degrees, especially from major universities. Competition will be strong.

Sociologist.   About 20,000 sociologists study group behavior and contribute to public relations, law enforcement, education, community planning, and more. The best positions call for a PhD, but there are jobs for master's and bachelor's graduates. PhD sociologists average about $37,000; in the federal government, they average about $40,000. Bachelor's graduates can expect to start at $15,000–18,000, master's graduates at $22,500. The job outlook is below average.

Urban and regional planner.   Urban and regional planners aid city, county, and state governments in selecting, siting, and building new medical, educational, and other facilities to meet the needs of the locality. They number 20,000, and most entry-level jobs require a master's degree or its equivalent in experience. The pay runs from $22,500 to over $40,000 a year. Employment should increase about as fast as the average for all occupations through the year 2000.

CAREERS IN THE LIFE SCIENCES

Many careers in the helping sciences deal in applications of the life sciences to human health. The helping sciences are thus applied versions of the life sciences, though they are not the only ones. The life sciences, the many branches of biology, can also be applied to agriculture and to industrial production. Every branch has both its results-oriented, applied side and its "pure," curiosity-satisfying basic research side.

However, the distinction between pure and applied work has far more to do with the setting and goal of one's work than with its content. That is, a pure research microbiologist will work to understand the lives of microorganisms. He or she may or may not teach, collect soil samples in the wilderness, or do other things. His or her lab may be in a university, a drug company, or a government agency. An applications-oriented microbiologist may work in the same places, or for a hospital or a public health agency. He or she will study microorganisms to find new antibiotics; to improve the production of beer, wine, or bread; or to find causes and treatments for diseases. Both pure and applied microbiologists work with the same organisms and the same techniques.

About a third of all life scientists work in research and development in business and industry, in government labs, and on campus. They must thus know research techniques and be able to use laboratory equipment and procedures. Over a third (37 percent) work in colleges and universities, where they may also do research. About a quarter are managers and administrators, running research programs, university departments, regulatory agencies, testing programs for foods and drugs, zoos, museums, and botanical gardens. The rest are inspectors of foods and drugs, consultants to business and government, technical writers, technical sales and service representatives, and others.

It may be simplest to approach the life science careers in terms of the many fields of biology, the specialties, a life scientist can move into. We cannot cover every biological specialty here, but we can discuss a few. More information is available in *Biology in Profile: A Guide to the Many Branches of Biology,* edited by P. N. Campbell for the International Council of Scientific Unions.

Later in this chapter, we will look at the careers available on campus, in industry and business, and in government. We will identify those areas where the pace of discovery is swift, the excitement of the workers is greatest, and the promise of the work for society is highest. Finally, we will list a few of the many organizations to which life scientists may belong and from which career information is available.

THE LIFE SCIENCES

The life sciences split into two broad fields that overlap to some extent. These fields are the biological sciences and the agricultural sciences.

Agricultural sciences

Agricultural scientists, numbering 46,000 in 1986, apply their knowledge of biology and other sciences to the production of food, fiber, and various other materials grown on farms. *Agronomists* work to improve the yield and quality of crops such as corn, soy beans, and cotton by developing new ways to grow them or to control pests such as weeds and insects; they also develop new varieties of crop plants. *Horticulturalists* do the same for orchard and garden plants, which are usually grown on a smaller scale, and add an emphasis on plants used in landscaping. *Animal scientists* focus on the breeding, growth, and care of farm animals; *veterinarians* are animal scientists whose purview includes pets, farm animals, and animals kept in zoos (see Chapter 4). Food technologists work to improve methods of processing, preserving, packaging, distributing, storing, and preparing foods; they work in basic research, applied research, and quality control.

Doctoral-level agricultural scientists can expect good employment opportunities through the year 2000, with starting salaries set at $27,000–33,000 per year in federal jobs in 1987. Bachelor's graduates will find more competition for jobs as well as lower pay, averaging annual salaries of $19,200 to start in private industry and $15,000–18,000 in the federal government.

Job opportunities in agricultural science may be greatest in private industry, for the rapid development of biotechnology (recombinant DNA genetic engineering) will soon be responsible for numerous agricultural products, some of which are already in the testing stage.

The prospects are not much different for workers in the related fields of forestry, range management, and soil conservation. *Foresters* plan and supervise the growing, protection, and harvesting of trees, which we use for fuel, lumber, paper, and even chemical feedstocks. They plant, map, inventory, and fight fire, pests, and disease. They may also deal in wild-life protection, watershed management, and the development and super-vision of camps, parks, and grazing lands. Most are employed by private industry. Due to intense job competition among foresters with no more than bachelor's degrees, higher degrees are advisable; they are essential for managerial, teaching, and research positions.

Soil conservationists help farmers and other land managers use their land as productively as possible without damaging it. They recommend the best uses of land and cultivation methods that will prevent erosion and maintain or improve fertility, monitor water supplies, and develop water conservation measures. Most have bachelor's degrees in agronomy, agricultural education, or general agriculture, or in related fields such as wildlife biology, forestry, or range management. *Range managers* work to improve and protect rangelands, or to maximize their use without damage. Rangelands are found mostly in the western United States, where they serve for animal grazing, wildlife habitats, water catchment areas, and recreation. Like foresters, range managers with ambitions for managerial, teaching, or research positions need graduate degrees.

These three occupations are lumped together by the U.S. Department of Labor as "Foresters and Conservation Scientists." Together, they con-tained some 23,000 workers in 1986, with over half working for the fed-eral Departments of Agriculture and the Interior. A fifth worked for state governments; six percent worked for municipalities. In 1986, fed-eral foresters averaged $32,800, range managers $28,500, and soil con-servationists $29,600; those in non-federal positions made somewhat less. In 1987, foresters, range managers, and soil conservationists with bachelor's degrees could enter federal employment at $14,800 per year. Holders of master's degrees could earn $22,500 per year. Doctorates could begin at $27,200 per year ($32,600 in research jobs).

For foresters and conservation scientists, employment should grow somewhat more slowly than the average for all occupations through the year 2000, largely because of federal budget constraints. Employment of soil conservationists will change very little, if at all. Growth in forestry and range management positions will occur only in the private sector, as private industry strives to increase its productivity.

Biological sciences

The job outlook for biological scientists is about the same as that for ag-ricultural scientists. The number of available positions should grow about as fast as the average for all occupations through the year 2000. Most growth in employment will be in private industry, especially in bio-technology firms. At the same time, the biological sciences are relatively recession-proof, since most jobs are in teaching, long-term research, and agriculture. In addition, a degree in the life sciences is excellent prepara-tion for a shift into the health fields.

Pay scales for biological scientists are roughly equivalent to those for agricultural scientists. A bachelor's graduate in biological science can expect $19,000 per year to start from private industry, $200 less than the agricultural bachelor's graduate can get. He or she can get $15,000–18,000 per year from the federal government. A master's graduate can start in the federal system at $18,000–22,000 per year and a doctorate can start at $27,000–33,000 per year.

Top-ranked researchers are in another ballpark entirely. The National Institutes of Health employ some 3,000 scientists in their laboratories. Those top-flight researchers who are civilians enjoyed salaries of $85,000 per year in 1988; those who belonged to the Public Health Service earned more. They could add up to another $50,000 from outside work such as consulting. But outside the government service, the rewards could be even greater: the chairman of a medical school department could, depending on his or her specialty, make between $200,000 and $300,000 per year. Not surprisingly, the NIH is having some trouble holding onto its best researchers.

The doctorate is essential for most positions in college teaching, independent research, and management. The master's will do for some jobs in applied research such as research assistant, field technician, or laboratory technician. A bachelor's degree qualifies one for some technician positions, for jobs in sales and service, and for support positions such as technical writer. High school biology teachers often have a bachelor's degree in biology, with added education courses.

Most of the 111,000 working biological scientists are less concerned with food, fiber, and raw material production than are agricultural scientists. They define their subject areas less in terms of human needs than in terms of life itself and the categories into which living things fall, or the levels of biological function. Biological scientists are thus zoologists and botanists, anatomists and physiologists and geneticists, and more.

Zoology is the scientific study of animals. It encompasses taxonomy or systematics, the identification, description, and classification of animals; mammalogy, the study of mammals; ichthyology, the study of fishes; herpetology, the study of reptiles; entomology, of insects; protozoology, of protozoa; and so on. A zoologist who emphasizes the economic impact of insects is an economic entomologist. One who studies disease-causing protozoa is a medical protozoologist. One who focuses on the interrelationships of animals with one another and with their environment is an ecologist. If one studies hormones one is an endocrinologist; behavior, an ethologist; parasites, a parasitologist; evolution, an evolutionary biologist. As an anatomist, one studies the structure of animals. As a physiologist, one focuses on growth, metabolism, reproduction, respiration, and movement. A geneticist studies genes and heredity. Biochemists and molecular biologists study the cell at the level of the molecules that comprise it.

Where the zoologist's concern is animals in all their aspects, the *botanist's* is plants. A botanist can specialize in single kinds of plants or in single aspects of their biology. Some botanists focus on ferns, mosses, or trees; on taxonomy, evolution, or genetics; on growth regulation, metabolism, photosynthesis, ecology, reproduction, or biochemistry.

Microbiology concentrates on microorganisms, on bacteria, yeasts, fungi, protozoa, and one-celled algae. The microbiologist too can be a taxonomist, geneticist, physiologist, ecologist, or evolutionary biologist. Often, he or she is interested in applications, for bacteria, yeasts, and fungi are used to produce foods such as wine, beer, bread, cheese, soy sauce, and tofu; antibiotics; and industrial chemicals. Equipped with new genes (recombinant DNA), microorganisms now produce hormones and other drugs for medical use. Since many microorganisms cause disease, some microbiologists are concerned with diagnosis, treatment, and prevention; they are medical microbiologists.

Physiology is concerned with how organisms work, how they respond to changes in their external and internal environments, in both health and disease. The physiologist thus seeks an understanding of the basic physical and chemical mechanisms of all of life. He or she not only wants to know what happens inside a plant, animal, or cell, but also how and why it happens. There are general, mammalian, comparative, plant, reproductive, and environmental physiologists, among others.

The *pharmacologist* is concerned with how drugs work. He or she is thus a kind of physiologist, but one with a bent toward health applications. Also a biochemist, he or she works with "pure" biochemists who use his or her understanding of drug action to probe the dynamics of cellular chemistry.

The *biochemist* studies the effects of foods, hormones, drugs, and toxins on plants, animals, and single cells. His or her aim is to know what chemical compounds make up living things and how they interact in metabolism, growth, reproduction, and heredity. He or she may be a basic researcher or an applied researcher working in medicine, agriculture, or industry. Many of today's biochemists work for biotechnology firms and strive to synthesize and produce on a large scale such biological chemicals as enzymes and antibiotics.

Ecology is concerned with the interrelationships between organisms and their environments. Interdisciplinary by nature, it encompasses many areas of biology, chemistry, geology, meteorology, and climatology. It contributes to our ability to understand and forestall disastrous effects of human activities, volcanic eruptions, and climate changes on our air, water, and food supplies. It also challenges our accustomed view of ourselves as independent of the world around us, and it has amply earned its sobriquet as "the subversive science."

Ethology is the study of animal behavior. Unlike psychology, it is more observational than experimental. It also seeks to understand the adaptive, evolutionary bases for human and animal actions.

Immunology is the study of how the body defends itself against invasion by foreign substances such as those carried on the surfaces of disease organisms and the cells of transplanted organs. Its greatest gift to medicine to date is vaccines, but it may have greater ones in store. Immunologists study the production of antibodies—proteins that attach to foreign molecules—and the activities of immune system cells that attack and kill foreign cells. From their efforts have come ways to produce pure antibodies (with "hybridomas") and stimulate or suppress the immune system. Soon, they may give us better treatments for cancer, more reliable organ transplants, and better relief from allergies. They may even find a way to treat and even cure viral infections such as herpes and AIDS (acquired immune deficiency syndrome); certainly, they are trying.

Genetics is the study of heredity, and geneticists have taught the world how to breed improved crop plants and animals. They were thus responsible for the "Green Revolution" that has helped to feed the burgeoning millions of the developing countries. Geneticists have also discovered the substance of the gene, DNA, and learned how to transplant genes from one organism to another. The study of DNA and its action is often better known as *molecular biology.* The gene transplant work has given rise to the promising field of genetic engineering, and genetic engineering companies have sprung up in the past decade to manufacture hormones, enzymes, and proteins for medical and industrial use. The future may yield crop plants that need less fertilizer, new foods, improved varieties of plants and animals, and cures for hereditary diseases.

Many geneticists remain basic researchers who study how various characteristics pass from parent to offspring. They usually study short-generation organisms such as viruses, bacteria, and fruit flies, although some study humans. *Human geneticists* have provided new explanations for such mental disorders as schizophrenia and depression. They are also concerned with the treatment and prediction of birth defects and heritable diseases such as Huntington's chorea. To aid this effort, some geneticists are now mounting a massive effort to map the human genome, identifying all human genes and pinning down their locations on the chromosomes. Others work as *genetic counselors,* advising people whose families have histories of genetic defects of their chances of having normal children.

There are many other fields of biological science, but those described above are enough to show the great breadth of the area and to suggest that a career here can have an enormous amount of variety. Most biological scientists split their time among research, teaching, administration, and writing. Some split theirs between university and industry or government. Others work full time for the government, an educational institution, a private research outfit, a zoo or botanical garden or museum. There are biologists everywhere, and they do just about everything that relates at all to life.

SCIENCE TECHNICIANS

Research in the life sciences, and in the earth, physical, space, and computer sciences, as well as engineering and mathematics, is not a matter only for PhD researchers. These men and women need the assistance of a horde of technicians who do much of the hands-on work of research. They design, build, and operate equipment, run tests, and process information. Outside of research, they work in product development, production, sales, and customer services; they also search for various resources (such as water, oil, and minerals) and help make them available for use.

In 1986, there were about 227,000 agricultural, biological, biomedical, chemical, forestry, geological, hydrological, meteorological, museum, nuclear, oceanographic, petroleum, and other science technicians (689,000 engineering technicians are counted separately; see Chapter 9). According to the Bureau of Labor Statistics, about 40 percent (in 1986) worked in manufacturing, largely in the food processing, chemical, and energy industries. Another 40 percent worked in academic settings and independent R&D laboratories. Less than a tenth worked for the federal government, largely in the Departments of Defense, Agriculture, Commerce, and the Interior. Overall, employment should increase about as fast as the average for all occupations through the year 2000.

Science technicians are qualified for their jobs by two-year degrees in specific technologies and by Armed Forces training programs. Bachelor's graduates with science backgrounds can also become technicians. In 1986, science technicians averaged about $22,000 per year, with a tenth earning less than $12,000 and a tenth earning over $36,000. Technicians in the life sciences earned less than those in the physical sciences. In 1987, federal pay began at $12,000–15,000, depending on education and experience.

THE HOT SPOTS

Where will most of the excitement lie in the life sciences for the next few years or decades? A great deal will come to the geneticists, biochemists, and molecular biologists who continue to develop the technology of genetic engineering. They will affect medicine, agriculture, and industry profoundly, and the inventions and processes they devise will make many of them wealthy. Some of the excitement will come to the immunologists who develop the methods to use purified antibodies and other techniques to attack now-intractable diseases such as AIDS and cancer, to purify raw materials in industry—even to purify sewage—and to ease the task of transplanting organs. More will accompany the effort to map the human genome. Great progress has been made in recent years in human evolution, neurophysiology, and endocrinology, and these fields too will spawn important discoveries. Other areas of the life sciences seem less promising for now, although if we increase our activities in space—and there are signs that we will—there will be a boom in the applications of physiology, immunology, ecology, microbiology, medicine, and other fields to the space environment.

Table 10   Estimated number of doctoral life scientists by type of position, 1985

Total	91,953
Academic sectors	53,976
Faculty	35,956
Professor	14,683
Associate professor	11,038
Assistant professor/instructor	7,860
Other	2,197
Nonfaculty	18,020
Postdoctorates	15,264
Other staff	2,756
Nonacademic sectors	37,977
Government	10,855
Industry	19,165
Other	7,957

Source: National Research Council and National Science Foundation

In most areas, the excitement will be less in the work than in the worker, for most biologists have always been drawn to their fields by factors like experiences with parents, early teachers, and mentors. They work more for the love of the work than for love of the consequences.

CAREERS ON CAMPUS

In 1985, 62 percent of all doctoral-level life scientists worked for educational institutions (see Tables 10 and 11 for breakdowns of life scientists by type of position and employment sector). Their pay was adequate, if not luxurious. In 1986–87, university instructors made an average of $21,300; assistant professors, $27,900; associate professors, $33,800; full professors, $45,500; and research technicians, about $20,000.

Growth in employment in the academic sector has slowed greatly in recent years. Between 1961 and 1965, full-time university faculty in-

Table 11   Employment sectors of life scientists with doctorate, 1985

	Educational institutions	Industry	Federal government
Biological scientists	40,688	9,337	5,049
Agricultural scientists	8,597	4,004	2,059
Medical scientists	24,893	5,824	1,581
Total	63,595	19,165	8,689

Source: National Research Council

creased by 13 percent; between 1973 and 1977, they grew by only 4 percent. The Department of Labor now projects faculty employment to decline until the mid-1990s. It will then begin to rise once more, although by 2000 employment will still be below that in 1986.

The reason for this pattern of stasis and decline is partly that during past growth periods, universities and faculties hired many new, young faculty members. But then the number of college students slowed its growth; in fact, a 20-percent decline in the number of 18-year-olds began in 1980 and will last until 1990. Institutions of higher education no longer needed to continue to expand their faculties and in fact began to look for ways to shrink their teaching staffs. Unfortunately, their faculty members were largely young and far from ready to retire. The result has been overemployment at some institutions; it should be no surprise that as those institutions bring their faculties better into line with demand, faculty employment must decline. It will begin to rise again only after demand—the number of 18-year-olds entering college—begins to increase once more.

Competition is thus stiff for relatively few jobs, though the situation *will* improve. Colleges and universities need less than 1,000 faculty members each year, and a single advertised position may draw hundreds of applicants. Many life scientists, with and without doctoral degrees, wind up teaching in high schools, which need about 3,000 new biology teachers every year.

Except in two-year schools, college and university life scientists are generally expected to be both teacher and researcher. However, their duties are hardly restricted to lecturing, supervising student laboratories, and doing their own research. They must also keep up with advances in their fields by reading and attending scientific meetings, write grant proposals to gain funding for their research, and write up the results of their research as papers and books. In addition, they must serve on various faculty committees.

College and university life scientists must have doctorates if they expect to advance beyond the level of instructor. Once they have obtained this degree, they may begin their working careers as "postdocs." They join the research team of a senior researcher in their field to concentrate on research and gain skills free from the demands of teaching and committee work.

The National Research Council (in *Postdoctoral Appointments and Disappointments)* calls the postdoc "an important period of transition between formal education and a career in research," a temporary job whose primary purpose "is to provide for continued education and experience usually, though not necessarily, under the supervision of a senior mentor. Included [in the definition] are appointments in government and industrial laboratories which resemble in their character and objectives postdoctoral appointments in universities. Excluded are appointments in residency training programs in the health professions."

However, many ex-postdocs say they were underpaid and exploited, and few women and minority people gain the positions. There were 4,470 bioscience postdocs in 1979, 10 times more than in 1972, and their average annual pay was only $12,000, less than two-thirds than that of their classmates already on faculties. By 1988, postdocs could expect pay in the instructor-assistant professor range of $20,000–30,000 per year. Most new bioscience PhDs plan on taking postdocs (in 1983, the figure was 70 percent), often because other, more desirable jobs are unavailable. They hope to have better luck later on, helped by the further training. The postdoc is thus very much a "holding pattern" for new PhDs, and its late start can set careers back seriously. Former postdocs never make as much money as their classmates, and their unemployment rate is about three times as high. Nevertheless, the postdoc can be very valuable to a career in research; 73 percent of new assistant professors in major research universities are former postdocs.

With or without a postdoc, a life scientist's first academic position may be that of instructor, perhaps while he or she is still a graduate student. Later come the positions of assistant professor, associate professor, and full professor and the job security of "tenure," which protects against arbitrary dismissal and relieves one of worrying over whether a contract will be renewed. On the way to the full professorship, many life scientists move from school to school around the country. It often seems that whether one works in academia, industry, or government, in any field, one's present employer never recognizes one's true worth. Promotion comes faster with a change in job.

Nonfaculty positions on campus also exist for life scientists. University and college medical centers and clinics employ the full range of health personnel. Museums hire naturalists, taxonomists, collectors, and curators. They focus on research, but they also teach courses to the general public (including students). *Curators* also administer their museums. *Museum exhibitors* conceive, plan, design, and set up the exhibits with which a museum speaks to the public; they are generalists well grounded in general biology, ecology, conservation, geology, geography, paleontology, anthropology, and principles of design. *Technical assistants* need only a bachelor's degree in biology.

Some universities are associated with their own or municipal zoos, botanical gardens, and arboretums. They employ veterinarians, plant and animal breeders, geneticists, ecologists, ethologists, and others who can help collect, preserve, and organize living and dead specimens from all over the world. Bachelor's and master's graduates may serve as gardeners, groundsmen, horticulturists, caretakers, animal keepers, exhibit preparers, writers, editors, and librarians. The pay is comparable to that for faculty members.

Private research laboratories may be on or near campus, affiliated with or run by one or more universities, or totally independent. The collection of labs at Research Triangle Park in North Carolina has a multi-university affiliation. The Jackson Laboratory in Bar Harbor, Maine, famed for its work in mouse genetics and cancer research, is totally independent. Private research laboratories hire life scientists of all kinds as researchers, technicians, and administrators. They provide a pleasant, stable work environment, and they pay as well as most universities.

CAREERS IN INDUSTRY

Where life scientists on campus teach and do basic and applied research, those who work for private companies in "industry" do mainly applied research. They seek answers with immediate, practical uses. Their purpose is to support their employers' efforts to make a profit.

Industry performs some three-quarters of this nation's research and development work. In 1988, it expected to spend about $62 billion on research and development (R&D), up 50 percent from 1980. In 1985, it employed about 500,000 R&D scientists and engineers, up 50 percent from 1975. The life sciences' share of these figures was considerable, since industry employs roughly a third of all life scientists. In 1980, the last year for which figures are available at this writing, industrial life science R&D spent $520 million on food and related products and $1,670 million on drugs and medicines. Many life scientists worked in production, sales, and management. The industries that hire life scientists include:

- Food processors.
- Plant and animal breeders and growers.
- Seed companies.
- Makers of agricultural chemicals, including pesticides, growth regulators, fertilizers, and dietary supplements.
- Pharmaceutical companies.
- Cosmetics makers.
- Wood growers, harvesters, and processors.
- Textile and leather makers and users.
- Petroleum products companies.
- Public utilities.
- Aerospace companies.
- Scholarly and textbook publishers.
- Makers of lab equipment and supplies.
- Collectors, growers, and processors of biological materials for classroom and lab use.
- Biological testing companies.
- Commercial medical labs.

The life scientists who work for these employers test for the effects on health of drugs, food additives, dyes, and chemicals; study the effects of construction and energy projects on the environment; strive to improve food production and processing; maintain quality control; and present information to the public. But they are not only researchers and technicians. Many companies put life scientists, especially those without doctorates, in sales, believing that people who understand a product and its uses can sell it more effectively and can communicate customer needs more precisely and usefully to the research staff. They use them in management too, believing that experts in a field are better able to oversee work in that field.

Most companies that employ life scientists have room for people with all degrees, and they often pay well. Early in the 1980s, one small Boston company, which supplied pure enzymes to research labs, employed four BS technicians at $12,000–15,000 per year, four PhD researchers at $27,000–32,000, and two PhD managers at $37,000–45,000. They were geneticists, molecular biologists, and biochemists.

A second company, this one in genetic engineering, employed eight MS technicians at $16,000–23,000 per year; 13 PhD researchers at $26,000–34,000; two managers at $18,000–22,500; and six "other" (perhaps upper management), with PhD, MA, and BA degrees, at $30,000–60,000. Their fields included microbiology, genetics, and molecular biology, and they had experience in gene cloning. Employees at both these companies are now making much more, for in the life sciences (as in many fields) pay goes up rapidly with experience.

The Upjohn Company is a large pharmaceutical corporation that employs nearly 8,000 people at its Kalamazoo, Michigan, headquarters and about 12,000 people nationwide. In 1985 it spent $280 million on R&D, almost double the budget for 1980. (Sales that year were over $2 billion.) The company makes drugs and agricultural and industrial chemicals, performs laboratory tests for physicians and hospitals, and provides health care personnel. In research, it employs biologists, biochemists, microbiologists, pharmacists, pharmacologists, physicians, and medical technologists. In "development and control," it employs pharmacists, microbiologists, and medical technologists. In manufacturing, it hires pharmacists. In sales, it uses biology, premedical, and pharmacy graduates. And in management, its president has an MD, one executive vice president has an MD and a PhD, and the vice president and general manager of the Agricultural Division is a veterinarian.

The pharmaceutical industry is very attractive to life scientists. Its activities are diverse; it depends utterly on its researchers for new products and continued success; and it gives its scientists practically everything they need in the way of equipment, materials, and technical assistance. It also allows—even urges—its people to collaborate with researchers in other fields and on campus and to publish scholarly papers and books.

All other industries deal in fewer products and offer less diversity. Most can afford fewer resources. But there are industrial positions for life scientists in virtually every field, with bachelor's, master's, or doctoral degrees, as researchers, technicians, managers, and salespeople.

CAREERS IN AND AROUND GOVERNMENT

Government is the nation's single largest employer. In 1984, the federal government employed 2,942,000 civilians, the states employed 3,898,000, and local governments employed 9,595,000. All levels of government together employed 16,436,000 of this country's 105 million employed civilians, or 15.7 percent of the labor force.

A great many scientists and engineers work for the public sector. In 1984, the federal government employed 307,000 of them, 39,000 of whom were life scientists. State and local governments and nonprofit institutions together employed similar numbers of scientists and engineers and of life scientists.

We will concentrate here on the federal system, for states and cities offer many of the same jobs. Unfortunately, states and cities do not pay quite as well as Uncle Sam, and they offer less generous fringe benefits such as sick leave, educational aid, vacations, insurance, and retirement pay. The people who work for the more local levels of government are often people who wish to live in a particular part of the country and are willing to forego income and other benefits in favor of lifestyle.

The federal government hires life scientists in every field to work in virtually every area of its operations. Some, but by no means all, of the agencies that use life scientists are:

Centers for Disease Control (CDC)

Central Intelligence Agency (CIA)

Department of Agriculture

Department of Commerce (National Bureau of Standards, National Oceanic and Atmospheric Administration)

Department of Defense

Department of Energy

Department of the Interior (National Park Service, U.S. Fish and Wildlife Service, Bureau of Land Management)

Department of Labor (Bureau of Labor Statistics, Occupational Safety and Health Administration [OSHA])

Department of Transportation

Environmental Protection Agency (EPA)

Food and Drug Administration (FDA)

National Aeronautics and Space Administration (NASA)

National Institutes of Health (NIH)

National Science Foundation (NSF)

Smithsonian Institution

Department of Veterans Affairs (VA)

Some concentrate on matters of health. The missions of NIH and CDC are disease-related research. The VA does medical research and delivers health care. OSHA monitors the workplace and enforces regulations designed to protect workers' health and safety. The FDA ensures the safety and efficacy of drugs and food additives. The EPA deals in part with environmental effects on health. The Department of the Interior deals with land and wildlife management, among other things; its state equivalents hire most game wardens.

Relatively few government programs other than those of NSF, NIH, and the Smithsonian deal much with basic biological research. Most direct their efforts to fulfilling missions assigned to them by Congress.

The GS grade system   Federal government jobs have GS (General Schedule) or other (GM, EC, EP, etc.) "grades" according to their difficulty and level of responsibility. Biological jobs have grades from GS-5 to GS-15; pay scales are set by grades, but government biologists are as well off as their industry colleagues and better off than their friends on campus.

The GS-5 grade is for white-collar workers with experience or education equivalent to a bachelor's degree. The GS-7 grade requires a bachelor's degree with a B average, top-third class rank, or elected membership in a national honorary society such as Phi Beta Kappa, or one year of professional experience, or one year of preprofessional student trainee experience. The GS-9 grade calls for two years of professional experience or graduate education, or a master's degree. GS-12 requires at least three years of professional experience with at least one year at a level of difficulty comparable to the GS-11 level. Higher grades depend on experience and excellence. In 1988, the annual pay range for grades GS-7–10 was $18,726–32,795; for GS-11–12, it was $27,716–43,181; for GS-13–15, it was $39,501–71,377. The "super grades"—GS16, 17, and 18—are for supervisory personnel such as agency directors; their pay peaked at $86,682 in 1988.

Further information is available from Federal Job Information centers, scattered around the country. Addresses are available in phone books and from local State Job Service or State Employment Security offices.

Federal employment has several advantages. One is the pay. Another is that under the protection of the civil service system, job security is good and there is ample opportunity for advancement. A third is that government employees may continue to receive full-time pay while continuing their education part-time (or full-time for up to one year). When they have finished the additional schooling, they are qualified for jobs at higher grade levels.

However, government biologists and other scientists have been fired or given unsatisfying assignments for revealing errors or publicly disagreeing with their superiors, who may be committed to a particular stance on controversial issues such as nuclear energy, abortion, or environmental protection regulation. (Legal protection for "whistleblowers" exists, but it seems ineffective.) Also, government employees are restrained from political activity; they cannot help in political campaigns, and to run for office themselves, they must quit their jobs.

Congressional fellows

Congress deals constantly with science and technology matters, and most senators and representatives have on their staffs people with scientific training and knowledge. These people may find their jobs through normal channels, or by knowing a member of Congress and helping out in campaigns or as an unpaid science adviser. Young PhDs may enter the congressional system through the Congressional Fellows Program run by the American Association for the Advancement of Science (AAAS). The fellows are sponsored for one year by individual scientific societies such as the AAAS itself, the American Society for Microbiology, the Biophysical Society, and the Federation of American Societies for Experimental Biology (FASEB) (nonbiological societies also take part in the program). The program began in 1973 with seven fellows.

In 1987, 15 organizations sponsored 36 Congressional Science and Engineering Fellows and Science, Engineering, and Diplomacy Fellows (who occupy positions in the U.S. Department of State and the U.S. Agency for International Development), selected on the basis of excellence and interest in science and public policy. The program's aim, in the words of the AAAS, is "to increase science-government interaction and to contribute to the policy-making processes of government."

The fellows begin their service with an intensive two-week orientation to government operations, focusing on issues involving science and public policy. For the next year, they then work in Congress and various government agencies while participating in a year-long seminar on public policy. Past fellows have worked on legislation concerning health policy, environmental regulation, and energy. After a year in Washington, they generally return to campus or industry, but some remain in Washington. They may continue their work for Congress, enter other sorts of government service, or even move toward high positions as heads of government agencies.

Lobbyists

It is also possible to work in Washington or in state capitals without being on a government payroll at all. Most companies and industries—including universities, scientific societies, and professional groups such as the American Medical Association—are vitally interested in government actions, in legislation, regulation, and policy formation. Quite naturally, they wish to influence these actions as much in their favor as they can. They thus provide information and opinion to legislators and bureaucrats. They cajole and persuade—they *lobby*—and their representatives, whether individuals or firms, are *lobbyists*.

On biological issues, the best lobbyists have some biological sophistication. They may be practicing researchers or physicians, lobbying part-time on their own or as representatives of their employers. They may also be biologists who have left their fields to lobby full time. They are all salespeople, and their function is exactly that of the sales force of a business; to explain technical matters clearly and to persuade the "customer" that the business deserves consideration and support.

Effective lobbyists are worth their weight in gold to industry. They can prevent a product ban, get a new product approved for sale, reduce the need to spend money on pollution control or safety equipment, and so on. They can mean millions to their employers, and they can be paid extremely well.

ORGANIZATIONS FOR LIFE SCIENTISTS

All fields of science have their scientific societies. These societies publish journals (which often carry help wanted ads) and hold annual meetings at which their members present papers and talk with one another. They also run job placement services, publish professional directories, and provide low-cost insurance and information on education and careers.

Some societies are multidisciplinary. The American Association for the Advancement of Science includes members in the life, earth, physical, and other sciences; it publishes the journal *Science,* which runs many job ads. Sigma Xi takes individual researchers as its members and publishes *American Scientist*. There are also many state and local "academies of science."

Some multidisciplinary societies are restricted to multiple disciplines within a single science; the American Medical Association and the Federation of American Societies for Experimental Biology are prominent examples. Most societies are both smaller and more restricted in their membership. State societies are restricted in geography, if not in fields. The American Association of Anatomists, American Society for Microbiology, American Physiological Society, Society of Systematic Zoology, and many more are restricted in field.

Many societies offer pamphlets on careers in their fields; Table 12 lists several with their addresses. The most helpful society may be the American Institute of Biological Sciences (AIBS), which publishes the semipopular magazine *Bioscience*, has a great deal of career information available, and (with the AAAS and FASEB) supports the Commission on Professionals in Science and Technology, an excellent source of employment and salary statistics.

Table 12 Societies and sources of further information for life scientists

AIBS
730 11th Street, NW
Washington, DC 20001-4584

Society of American Foresters
5400 Grosvenor Lane
Bethesda, MD 20814

American Society of Icthyologists and Herpetologists, Inc.
Florida State Museum
University of Florida
Gainesville, FL 32611

American Ornithologists' Union
Society of Systematic Zoology
   National Museum of Natural History
   Washington, DC 20560

American Society of Mammalogists
Department of Zoology
Brigham Young University
Provo, UT 84602

American Society of Biological Chemists
American Physiological Society
American Institute of Nutrition
American Society for Pharmacology and Experimental Therapeutics, Inc.
   9650 Rockville Pike
   Bethesda, MD 20814

National Association of Science Writers, Inc.
PO Box 294
Greenlawn, NY 11740

American Medical Association
535 North Dearborn Street
Chicago, IL 60610

American Osteopathic Association
Department of Public Relations
142 East Ontario Street
Chicago, IL 60611

American Society of Agronomy
677 S. Segoe Rd.
Madison, WI 53711

AAAS
1333 H Street NW
Washington, DC 20005

American Association of Museums
1225 I Street NW
Suite 200
Washington, DC 20005

Botanical Society of America
Dr. David L. Dilcher, Secretary
Dept. of Biology
Indiana University
Bloomington, IN 47405

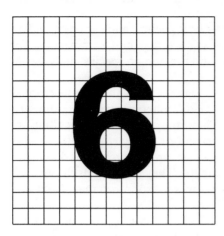

CAREERS IN THE EARTH SCIENCES

Where the helping and social sciences deal with human beings and their health and behavior, and the life sciences deal with all living things, the earth sciences deal with the only home of life that we know: the Earth. That is, they deal with the environment of life, and they are in fact also called the environmental sciences.

It should thus not be surprising to find that there is some overlap between certain of the earth sciences and the life sciences. This overlap is greatest where the earth sciences address portions of the Earth where living things abound, such as the oceans, lakes, rivers, and soil. There is also overlap between the life sciences and studies of climate and geography, the earth science that focuses on the Earth's surface and the resources it bears. There is very little overlap between the life sciences and those earth sciences that best fit the image that "earth science" first brings to mind: geology and geophysics address the planet's rocks, the movements of continents, the eruptions of volcanoes, and the shudderings of earthquakes.

The earth sciences employ some 80,000 men and women, not counting technicians. These people are not known as earth scientists, but as geologists, geochemists, geophysicists, geographers, limnologists, climatologists, meteorologists, oceanographers, hydrologists, and so on. Let us then look at the earth sciences one by one, starting with geography, the very first science most people ever encounter, and for too many the last.

GEOGRAPHY

As taught in elementary and junior high school, geography deals with the nations and regions of the Earth, their lands and waters, peoples and products, imports and exports. It is a social science, a life science, and an earth science. It is, perhaps, the one science that best summarizes, for pedagogic purposes, the entire world and the human species' activities in that world.

As practiced, geography is equally comprehensive, though the emphasis is more practical than pedagogic. Geographers strive to explain why and how people live where they do. They study the nature, distribution, and interaction of the many characteristics of the Earth's surface, especially as these pertain to human needs. They are researchers and analysts on campus, in industry, and in government. They teach, consult, and advise. They are planners and administrators of resource management and economic development.

Their tools are climate records, resource inventories, and soil and water analyses. They gather information from maps, aerial photographs, and Earth-surveying satellites. Because they need sophisticated statistics and advanced mathematics to analyze their data and build explanatory models, they need powerful computers.

Economic geographers concentrate on the distribution of a region's economic activities—forestry, agriculture, mining, and manufacturing—and may advise private firms and governments on where best to locate new facilities. *Political geographers* focus on how political entities fit the land, describing and defining natural boundaries such as rivers and mountain ranges for nations, states, and cities. *Urban geographers* restrict their concerns to cities and their surrounding areas; they may advise in such areas as community and industrial development.

Physical geographers emphasize water systems, landforms, vegetation patterns, wildlife distribution, climate, and other physical aspects of the Earth's surface; they contribute to decisions on defense, conservation, agriculture, transportation, marketing, health, and more. *Regional geographers* deal with the physical, political, and economic geography of a region, such as New England or Michigan's Upper Peninsula; to work effectively, they must also understand local language, culture, history, and customs.

Cartographers compile and interpret geographic data, with the aid of computers, and design and prepare maps. *Medical geographers* deal with the effects of environment (water, air, climate, soil, vegetation) on health. Often concerned with trace elements such as fluoride or selenium, or with air and water pollution, they work with public health departments and statisticians to determine environmental effects on health and find causes of diseases.

Other specialties include satellite data interpretation, location analysis, conservation, geographic methods and techniques, and agricultural, cultural, historical, population, rural, and social geography.

Many of the nation's geographers spend their days comfortably indoors. Many more work in the field, as members of multidisciplinary research teams. They may travel to remote parts of the world, and they may need considerable adaptability (to adjust to different cultures) and physical stamina.

In 1980, there were about 15,000 geographers, according to the Bureau of Labor Statistics. By the time of the 1988–89 edition of the *Occupational Outlook Handbook,* which reported employment in each field as of 1986, geographers were not being counted separately from the category of "social scientists and urban planners," which encompassed almost 200,000 people in several areas (see Chapter 4). We can estimate that the number of geographers in 1986 was probably in the neighborhood of 17,000.

Jobs exist in geography for people with bachelor's, master's, and doctoral degrees. A bachelor's degree is enough to teach geography in the public school system, and it can qualify one for entry-level jobs in government and industry. Bachelor's geographers with no experience started with the federal government at $14,800 to $18,400 a year in 1987. Future bachelor's geographers can expect intense competition for the relatively few jobs available. Specialists in cartography, planning, and satellite data interpretation face the best prospects.

A master's degree qualifies one for community college teaching and aids advancement greatly in industry and government. Specialists in applied areas can expect good job prospects in planning and marketing. In 1987, the federal government paid new master's graduates with no experience $22,500.

A PhD is essential for most teaching and research positions at colleges and universities, as well as for senior positions in government and industry. The pay for geographers with doctorates is much better, starting at $27,200 per year with the federal government.

The job forecast for doctoral geographers is best for industrial and government research and administrative posts. The best chances on campus are for those who have specialized in quantitative research techniques, computer mapping, and natural resource management.

GEOLOGY

The classic portrait of a geologist is a rock hound with a pick and hammer in his or her hands. The modern geologist uses the same tools, but also explosives and seismic recorders to chart the layers of rock deep below the surface and deep-drilling rigs to retrieve samples from the depths. Both the classic and modern geologist are students of the Earth's crust. They study structure, composition, and history. They want to know what rocks exist where, how they were formed, and how and why they have moved and changed since their formation. They locate mineral deposits, prepare maps, conduct geologic surveys, and advise on the suitability of construction sites.

Economic geologists seek minerals and solid fuels. *Petroleum geologists* seek oil and natural gas deposits. *Marine geologists* study the ocean bottoms. *Engineering geologists* concentrate on construction sites for dams, highways, tunnels, and the like. *Mineralogists* classify and analyze minerals and jewels. *Geochemists* work on the chemical processes that have formed and transformed rocks and laid down mineral deposits. *Volcanologists* focus on volcanoes and strive to predict their eruptions. *Geomorphologists* study the forms of the land's surface and the forces of erosion, glaciation, volcanic eruption, and seismic uplift that have shaped those forms. *Paleontologists* are primarily concerned with the traces of past life (fossils) found in the Earth's rocks. *Geochronologists* seek the ages of rocks and landforms by studying the decay of radioactive elements. *Stratigraphers* study the layers (strata) of rock in the Earth's crust in terms of sequence and mineral and fossil content.

Most of the nation's 52,000 geologists and geophysicists spend large amounts of time in the field, but they work in labs and offices. Most work for petroleum, mining, quarrying, and construction firms, and it is in the resource industries that the job prospects of geologists look best. Unfortunately, employment seems likely to grow more slowly than the average for all occupations, unless a new energy crisis develops. A bachelor's degree qualifies one for many entry-level positions, but a doctorate is essential for advancement, as well as for college and university teaching and research positions.

In 1986, new bachelor's graduates in geology started at an average of $19,200. This starting salary is one of the few to show an actual decline since 1980, when graduates in this field received over $1,000 more to start; the reason is the decline in the petroleum industry due to falling prices of imported oil. In 1986, federal geologists averaged $37,500 per year. In 1987, bachelor's geologists could start with the federal government at $14,822 or $18,358; master's geologists could start at $18,358 or $22,458; doctoral geologists could begin at $27,172 or $32,567.

GEOPHYSICS

Like geologists, geophysicists study the physical structure of the Earth, but they range both more broadly and more deeply. They exploit the planet's electric, magnetic, and gravitational fields to probe the molten core, study and explain the planet's shape, and map past motions of the continents. Computers and satellites are among their essential tools, as are magnetometers, seismometers, gravimeters, and drilling rigs.

The American Geophysical Union classifies as geophysicists both oceanographers and atmospheric scientists (including meteorologists). However, we will here treat those specialties separately (see below). The Union also claims the study of other planets for its own, but despite the justice of the claim—the same techniques and theories are applicable to all planets, no matter how distant—we will cover the space sciences in Chapter 8.

Like geography and geology, geophysics has numerous subfields or specialties. *Solid earth geophysicists* seek oil and mineral deposits, study earthquakes, and map the planet. *Exploration geophysicists* also seek oil and minerals. Both use seismic techniques (bouncing sound waves off subsurface structures), magnetic techniques (seeking changes in the Earth's magnetic field), and gravimetric techniques (seeking perturbations of the Earth's gravitational field due to underground concentrations or deficiencies of mass).

Seismologists study earthquakes, using the sound waves they emit to find their sources and describe the subsurface features that generate them; in the last few years, they have actually begun to map the Earth's core. Seismologists also generate their own sound waves to explore for oil and minerals and to analyze the strength and stability of the soil and rock beneath construction sites. *Geodesists* study the planet's size and shape and its gravitational field in order to increase the precision of maps; they find careful study of perturbations in the orbits of satellites very useful. *Hydrologists* study the distribution, flow, and composition of underground and surface waters; some address problems of water supply, irrigation, erosion, and flood control. *Geomagneticians* deal with the Earth's magnetic field. *Paleomagneticians* describe the way that field has changed in past aeons; they can do so because the planet's rocks record the direction of the field at the times of their formation. *Petrologists* study the strengths, chemical compositions, and crystal structures of rocks.

Yet all these subfields of geophysics deal only with pieces of the whole. People who crave the big picture, who want to grasp the planet all at once, can become *tectonophysicists* and deal with the study of plate tectonics. This subfield examines the processes that drive the motions of the planet's crust: seafloor spreading, continental drift, the subduction of crustal slabs in oceanic trenches, the thrusting of slabs into, over, and past each other to fold up mountain ranges and drive volcanoes and earthquakes. Tectonophysicists thus address the strength, elasticity, rigidity, and thermal properties of the Earth's crustal materials, and they share the concerns of petrologists, seismologists, volcanologists, geochemists, geologists, and geo- and paleomagneticians.

In 1986, new bachelor's graduates in geophysics started at an average of $19,200. This starting salary, like that for geologists, is one of the few to show an actual decline since 1980, when graduates in this field received over $1,000 more to start, all due to the decline in the petroleum industry, which in turn was due to falling prices of imported oil. In 1986, federal geophysicists averaged $40,900 per year, doing a little better than geologists. In 1987, bachelor's geophysicists could start with the federal government at $14,822 or $18,358; master's geophysicists could start at $18,358 or $22,458; doctoral geophysicists could begin at $27,172 or $32,567.

Employment should grow more slowly than the average for all occupations through the year 2000, since energy companies have cut back on their search for minerals, oil, and gas. Job prospects will, however, improve eventually, for when petroleum grows scarce—as it inevitably must—the search for new supplies will require many geologists and geophysicists.

OCEANOGRAPHY

The realm of the oceanographer covers over two-thirds of the Earth's surface. It is the oceans, rich with food, covering vast deposits of minerals and fossil fuels, birthplace of storms, highway for ships. Here, oceanographers study tides, winds, currents, fish, seaweed, and the sediments, valleys, and mountain ranges of the ocean floor. Their work aids weather prediction, fisheries, resource discovery and retrieval, and national defense. Their tools are ships, aircraft, satellites, drills, nets, dredges, cameras, maps, computers, and even land-based labs.

Biological oceanographers, close kin to marine biologists, deal with the life of the oceans; they study the life cycles, ecologies, and migrations of fish and unravel the manifold effects of marine pollution. *Physical oceanographers* concentrate on nonbiological aspects of the seas, such as tides, winds, currents, upwellings, and temperature patterns. *Geological oceanographers* study the portion of the Earth's crust that lies beneath the oceans. *Chemical oceanographers* concentrate on the chemical composition of and the chemical reactions in seawater and seabottom sediments. *Oceanographic engineers* design and build the tools and instruments for oceanographic research; they also work on undersea construction projects, as in the laying of cables and the building of oil-drilling platforms. *Limnologists* are freshwater "oceanographers."

Oceanography is a relatively small field. There were only about 3,000 oceanographers in 1986. Over half worked on campus, a quarter for the federal government, and the rest for industry. Bachelor-level oceanographers were beginners, technicians, or laboratory assistants. A doctorate is necessary for most high-level positions, especially in research and teaching.

The oceanographer's pay is similar to that of other earth scientists. In 1986, federal oceanographers averaged $38,000 a year. In 1987, new bachelor's graduates began in federal service at $14,800 or $18,400; new master's graduates began at $22,500; and new doctorates began at $27,200 or $32,600.

Jobs for oceanographers should grow at about the average rate through the year 2000. Doctoral-level oceanographers will face the best prospects; oceanographers with lesser degrees may be able to find jobs only as research assistants or technicians.

METEOROLOGY

Meteorologists are concerned with the phenomena that take place in the Earth's blanket of air, the atmosphere. That is, with the aid of data obtained from satellites, aircraft, and ground stations, they study winds, clouds, temperature patterns, and precipitation. They strive to understand the physical nature of the atmosphere, its motions and processes, and the ways it affects the surface of the planet, perhaps especially those parts occupied by humans. One of their prime concerns is thus the understanding and prediction of weather.

Operational meteorologists specialize in weather forecasting. They use data on atmospheric movement, temperature, humidity, air pressure, and cloud content to make short-term and long-term predictions. Because of the complexity of the atmosphere, they rely greatly on computer models of the atmosphere, but even the best models and computers allow only short-term predictions with any accuracy. Long-term predictions are necessarily imprecise; the National Weather Service's 30-day projections, for instance, say only whether temperature and precipitation will be above or below average. ("Astrological" meteorologists, who believe that the positions of the planets in the sky affect weather patterns on Earth, claim much better accuracy than traditional meteorologists, even in the long term—though such claims are questionable at best.)

Physical meteorologists study the physical and chemical properties of the atmosphere. They probe the upper atmosphere with balloons and sounding rockets, fly data-gathering aircraft through clouds and hurricanes, and—from safe distances—study tornadoes. They want to know why clouds and storms form, why rain and snow fall when and where they do, why and how changes in ocean surface temperature affect the weather, and more. Their results are clearly of great value to weather forecasting. Their studies may also soon be of great interest to all who worry about sun-induced skin cancer, for it is physical meteorologists who study the loss of the ultraviolet-blocking stratospheric ozone layer.

Climatologists are interested in long-term weather patterns, or climate. By studying an area's past weather records, they define the area's climate. Changes in past and present patterns—a warming, a cooling, or an increase or decrease in precipitation—then lead them to the causes of climate change, from shifts in the Earth's orbit to changes in the sun's output of heat to volcanic clouds. Climatologists are very useful in land use planning, building design, and the planning of heating and cooling systems. They also help predict the effects of human activities on future climate; recently, climatologists have been intensely studying the warming of the planet that must follow from the release of carbon dioxide due to the burning of fossil fuels and the increase of the greenhouse effect.

Most people think of meteorologists in terms of television and radio weather forecasters. However, these people often do little more than report forecasts made by other meteorologists, such as those employed by the National Weather Service. Of the nation's 6,600 meteorologists, one-third work for the federal government, 1,800 for the National Oceanic and Atmospheric Administration, and 250 for the Department of Defense. (The military employs thousands of its personnel in meteorological work.) The rest work for commercial airlines, weather consulting firms, aerospace firms, and other private enterprises. TV and radio are only the visible tip of the iceberg.

A bachelor's degree is the minimum essential for an entry-level job in weather forecasting. In 1987, bachelor's graduates could start with the federal government at $14,822 or $18,358 per year. Advanced degrees are necessary for research, teaching, and supervisory and administrative positions. The federal government pays a beginning master's graduate $18,358 or $22,458 and a new doctorate $27,172 or $32,567. The average federal meteorologist earned $39,700 in 1986.

Jobs for meteorologists should grow faster than the average for all occupations through the year 2000. The best job prospects will be in private industry and for those with advanced degrees. In addition, the National Weather Service will provide many openings as it strives to improve its weather forecasting.

THE HOT SPOTS

The hottest areas in the earth sciences relate to energy, natural resources, ozone, and climate. Tectonophysics, volcanology, and seismology are active fields. So is long-term weather forecasting, for bigger and faster computers will soon be available, and meteorologists will be devising better, more comprehensive models to take advantage of the new machines.

The hottest spots of all may lie where the earth sciences impinge on the space sciences. Satellites have proven of immense value to weather forecasting and to surveys of the Earth's surface (for mapping, seeking mineral deposits, and appraising human activities such as agriculture, urban spread, and new construction). They have also helped extend the purview of earth scientists to other planets, as have spacecraft such as the two Viking craft that visited Mars; by providing comparative data, they have aided the understanding of processes on Earth itself. However, missions to other planets have slowed drastically and may not resume until the 1990s or later. Earth-watching satellites will remain valuable, and related jobs may burgeon.

CAREERS ON CAMPUS

A smaller percentage of doctoral earth scientists than of doctoral life scientists work on campus (see Table 13). Their jobs, however, are similar in that they teach, do research, and earn comparable pay. They may also work in museums and in nearby affiliated or unaffiliated private research outfits. Many academic earth scientists are also consultants to industry; they may earn more in this capacity than they earn from their primary employer.

Table 13 Employment of doctorate earth scientists, 1985

	Educational institutions	Industry	Federal government
Geologists and geophysicists	5,059	4,769	2,414
Ocean and atmospheric scientists	2,163	485	1,045

Source: National Research Council

CAREERS IN INDUSTRY

Industry now employs less than a third of all earth scientists. The energy and mining industries dominate the field, but many others also employ geologists, cartographers, geophysicists, meteorologists, and oceanographers. They use them to find fossil fuels and minerals and work out the best techniques for extracting them, to prepare maps, and to forecast weather. Many geographers work for text and map publishers, travel agencies, and insurance companies. Many earth scientists wind up in management and sales positions. The pay tends to be more liberal in industry than on campus or in government.

CAREERS IN GOVERNMENT

Of the 307,000 scientists and engineers employed by the federal government in 1984, 17,000 were earth scientists. The number of earth scientists is about the same now, and they include geographers, geologists, geochemists, geophysicists, oceanographers, meteorologists, and all their subfields.

The federal government employs earth scientists in the National Oceanic and Atmospheric Administration and its National Weather Service, in the Bureau of Mines and U.S. Geological Survey of the Department of the Interior, in the National Bureau of Standards, in the National Science Foundation, and in the Departments of Defense and Energy. Still others work for NASA, the EPA, and the Departments of Agriculture and Transportation. Their functions are as described earlier in this chapter.

Earth scientists can also work as congressional fellows and staff scientists and as lobbyists. In such positions, they work to supply reliable advice to members of Congress; as lobbyists, they may strive to persuade Congress to fund particular energy development or research projects.

ORGANIZATIONS FOR EARTH SCIENTISTS

Like life scientists, earth scientists can belong to numerous professional societies, many of which offer career information and help in finding jobs. The multidisciplinary societies to which earth scientists may belong include the American Association for the Advancement of Science, Sigma Xi, and local and state academies of science. More specialized societies are listed in Table 14.

Job announcements appear in *Science* (AAAS); in *EOS,* the weekly news magazine of the American Geophysical Union; and in the monthly newsletter of the American Meteorological Society. The Geological Society of America runs a computer matching service for job seekers (GSA Employment Matching Service, 2300 Penrose Place, Boulder, CO 80301).

Table 14 Societies and sources of further information for earth scientists

Association of American Geographers 1710 16th Street NW Washington, DC 20009	Society of Exploration Geophysicists P.O. Box 70240 Tulsa, OK 74170
American Geological Institute 4220 King Street Alexandria, VA 22302	American Meteorological Society 45 Beacon Street Boston, MA 02108
American Geophysical Union 2000 Florida Avenue NW Washington, DC 20009	American Littoral Society (Oceanography) Sandy Hook Highlands, NJ 07732

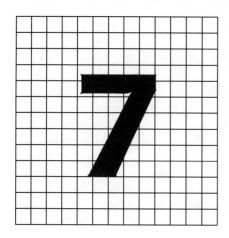

CAREERS IN THE PHYSICAL SCIENCES

The physical sciences are chemistry, physics, and their offspring, materials science. Putting things as simply as possible, chemistry is the study of the interactions of atoms and molecules, while physics is the study of the behavior of single atoms and their component pieces, of large assemblages of matter—crystals and bricks, liquids and gases, planets and stars—and of energy. Materials science deals with surfaces, catalysts, alloys, crystals, and production techniques for such devices as the microminiaturized (integrated) electronic circuits or chips that make personal computers, digital watches, and many other modern devices possible.

The physical sciences thus deal with neither life nor the environment but with the components of both. Their domain is matter in all its forms, energy, and the interactions of the two. They generate knowledge crucial to our understanding of the universe and essential to all other fields of science. They are at the roots of technology and engineering, and their fruits saturate our daily lives. They thus absorb the interests of over 140,000 men and women, nearly twice as many as the earth sciences.

Physical scientists work in both basic and applied research. Relatively few teach on campus. Most work for industry, in research and development. Average incomes are thus high, and there are jobs for people with all levels of education, even for brand-new high school graduates.

CHEMISTRY

Chemistry is the science of substances, the study of atoms and molecules, elements and compounds. Chemists break matter down to learn its components, and they put components together to make new substances. They study the ways in which the components go together in chemical reactions and the ways in which they can fall apart again. They have invented synthetic materials such as nylon, polyethylene, and other plastics; additives to preserve food and enhance lubricants; methods to convert the useless gunk that is raw petroleum into free-flowing gasoline; and much, much more. They work in the textile, food, energy, electronics, glass, paper, packaging, machinery, cosmetics, paint, drug, and chemical industries, and in more. They are almost as ubiquitous as life scientists, and they may be more essential to civilization as we know it.

Three-fifths of the nation's 105,000 chemists work in industry, many in research and development and the rest in production, quality control, management, sales, and even finance. They may also work in advertising, public relations, environmental protection, and industrial safety and health departments. They may be writers, editors, and patent agents and attorneys.

In 1986, 19,000 chemists taught in colleges and universities. Half that number worked for the federal government, the rest worked for state and local governments. Government chemists also do research and development work, but many are in safety and health and environmental protection as inspectors and regulators. On campus, chemists concentrate on teaching and research.

Like most sciences, chemistry can be broken into several subfields. The major ones are biochemistry, physical chemistry, organic chemistry, inorganic chemistry, and analytical chemistry. *Biochemists* deal with the chemistry of living things, with proteins, fats, starches, DNA, and drugs (see Chapter 5).

Physical chemists are concerned with the physical properties of matter. They strive to describe, in rigorous mathematical terms, the conversion of solid to liquid and liquid to gas (and vice versa). They study the statistics of molecular interactions, and their work on combustion and on the plasmas ("gases" of ions) that will one day provide fusion power contributes to the improvement of existing and the development of new energy sources.

Organic chemists focus on carbon-containing (organic) compounds, such as those produced by living organisms. They thus work in the petroleum, coal, wood products, plastics, textiles, and food industries. They devise new synthetic materials and new production processes for old materials. They convert one material into another, as in their work on turning the hydrocarbons locked into oil shale into fuel or on turning the waste products of the paper industry into feedstocks for chemical and plastic plants. They also study the ways in which carbon combines with other substances.

Inorganic chemists focus on non-carbon-containing compounds. They find employment in the mining industries, where ores must be broken down to retrieve pure metals and other substances. They work in the electronics industry, devising materials and methods for the construction of solid-state electronic components such as integrated circuits. They devise inorganic catalysts for both organic and inorganic reactions, as for the production of ammonia (for fertilizer) and methane (synthetic natural gas), for the liquefaction and gasification of coal, and for the removal of pollutants from automobile and factory exhausts.

Analytical chemists analyze. Using chemical tests, gas chromatographs, spectroscopes, and other sophisticated equipment, they seek the exact composition of substances. They are crucial to industrial quality control, for they check the purity of raw materials and finished products. Often, they are troubleshooters; a textile plant's color or dye chemist, faced with a problem such as the failure of a dye to stick to a fabric, may analyze drying agents, dyes, and other materials to find a solution.

Analytical chemists are also important in government, for they monitor air and water pollution and food and drug purity. Some work as forensic chemists for police departments and the FBI. They develop evidence in criminal cases by analyzing samples of blood, saliva, and other body fluids; soils; fibers; and other substances.

It is possible to classify chemists in narrower terms. Job descriptions often name forensic, food, color, dye, paper, and petroleum chemists; environmental chemists; development chemists; and quality control or assurance chemists. However, the broader classification by function and approach instead of by job seems more useful to anyone who is looking for a career.

Chemists generally work on a relatively small scale, using milligrams or grams of material in labs fitted with test tubes, beakers, distillation columns, flasks, stirrers, heaters, lasers, and electronic equipment. *Chemical engineers,* whose job is to turn laboratory processes into industrial production, work on a much larger scale, with ton lots of raw material and acres of vats and pipes. We will consider them in more detail in Chapter 9.

Chemists with doctoral degrees are qualified for college and university teaching and research positions and for industrial and government research and administration posts. A master's degree is enough for many jobs in applied research and for some college and community college teaching positions. A bachelor's degree will do for many beginning jobs as research assistant, product tester or analyst, and technical sales or service representative.

According to the U.S. Department of Labor, the job prospects for chemists will be best in the pharmaceuticals and biotechnology industries. Employment in the petrochemical and most manufacturing industries will be relatively static. Overall, employment is expected to expand more slowly than the average for all occupations through the year 2000.

Still, pay is and will continue to be good. In 1986, senior supervisory chemists averaged over $74,000. The American Chemical Society reports that in that year, bachelor's degree chemists averaged $33,000 per year, master's chemists averaged $37,900, and doctorate chemists averaged $47,800. Starting salaries were, of course, lower, averaging $23,400 for bachelor's graduates, $28,000 for master's graduates, and $36,400 for new doctorates. Federal pay ran somewhat lower, with federal chemists averaging $38,600 in 1986.

PHYSICS

Physicists consider themselves the most fundamental of scientists, for they are the ones who work out the basic laws of nature. They study the nature and behavior of atoms and their components (electrons, protons, and neutrons) and of the components of electrons, protons, and neutrons—kaons, pions, muons, and quarks, among others. They study what happens when atoms and subatomic particles break down and assemble, how they react to collisions with each other and to electromagnetic radiation. They study the flow of electrons in solids, of light in space, and of water in pipes. They apply the laws of classical mechanics to studies of how objects fall, orbit, and bang together; those of quantum mechanics to studies of subatomic particles; and those of Einstein's relativity theory to studies of objects at great distances in space and at very high speed. Always, they use mathematics to understand, explain, and predict, and their theories are equations. Almost always, they apply their predictions and theories to other fields—to chemistry, biology, geophysics, and engineering; to communications, transportation, electronics, and health.

There were some 36,000 physicists in this country in 1986. A fifth worked for the federal government, over a third (14,000) were college and university teachers, and the rest worked for industry, mostly for defense-related companies, aircraft and instrument makers, and electrical equipment companies.

Some physicists actually work in health-related fields. *Biophysicists* apply the laws of physics to biological systems, studying vision, hearing, nerve action, blood flow, and even the behavior of DNA. *Health physicists* are concerned with the effects of radiation and radioactive materials on biological systems. *Medical physicists* study the use of ionizing (nuclear, X-ray) and thermal radiation in diagnosis and treatment, methods of recording and interpreting the electrical activity of the brain and heart, and the use of high frequency sound. They design, build, and use ultrasound, CAT (computerized axial tomography), PET (positron emission tomography), and MRI (magnetic resonance imagery) scanners that construct images of the interior of the body.

The more traditional varieties of physicists steer clear of biology. *Solid-state physicists* study metals, alloys, ceramics, semiconductors, and insulators, contributing most to metallurgy, engineering, and electronics. *Nuclear physicists* focus on the interior of the atom with cyclotrons and larger particle accelerators; they are responsible for bombs, power plants, and radioactive tracers invaluable in medical diagnosis. *Elementary particle physicists* extend the nuclear physicist's purview to the components of the components of the atom; the applications of these subcomponents so far are few, but they promise a unified view of the universe and perhaps new energy sources, transportation methods, and more. *Atomic, molecular,* and *electron physicists* study how electrons and nuclei interact, how atoms combine as molecules, and how the electrons of atoms and molecules respond to radiation; they help chemists understand chemical reactions, and they have birthed the technique of spectroscopy, whereby tiny amounts of substances can be identified by the light they give off when heated.

Optical physicists study light and design lenses and lasers. *Acoustical physicists* focus on sound and contribute to the design of microphones, speakers, tape decks, and hearing aids. *Fluid physicists* deal with the flow of liquids and gases and help design cars, jet engines, and plumbing systems. *Plasma physicists* study electrically charged fluids, or plasmas; many are involved in current attempts to make fusion energy work. *Planetary physicists* are geophysicists under another name that lets them study other worlds as well as the Earth. *Space physicists* study the regions beyond the atmosphere; *astrophysicists* and *cosmologists* study stars and the universe; with planetary physicists, they are all space scientists, whom we will discuss in Chapter 8.

Any physicist can be either an *experimentalist* or a *theoretician.* The theoreticians almost invariably have doctorates. So do most of the experimentalists, since the doctorate is essential for college and university teaching and research, for upper-level research positions in government and industry, and for higher administrative positions. Physicists with master's degrees can find some research and teaching positions. Those with only bachelor's degrees can get into applied research and development or into jobs as research assistants or technicians. Many bachelor's graduates work in design, administration, and engineering.

In 1986, industry started its master's-level physicists at $31,200 per year and its doctoral physicists at $42,500 per year, on the average. The federal government in 1987 started bachelor's graduates at $14,822 or $18,358 per year, master's graduates at $18,358 or $22,458 per year, and doctorates at $27,172 or $32,567 per year. In 1986, federal physicists averaged $45,600.

The employment of physicists is expected to grow about as fast as the average for all occupations through the year 2000, but actual growth will depend heavily on how research and development expenditures grow. The best opportunities will be related to electronics, energy, defense, and perhaps space, especially if the latter two continue to be combined in the Strategic Defense Initiative (SDI).

MATERIALS SCIENCE

Materials science focuses heavily on the properties of the substances people use in various devices. It is thus strongly weighted toward physics, perhaps especially toward solid-state physics and the manipulation of electronic materials, as in the etching of circuits on silicon chips with ultraviolet, X-ray, and electron beams.

However, materials scientists include *crystallographers,* who study the ways atoms pack together in crystalline and noncrystalline (amorphous) solids and in thin films, membranes, fibers, glasses, liquids, and gases. Their work contributes to the electronics industry, to the conversion of sunlight to electricity with photovoltaic cells, to the understanding of how radiation affects the structural materials of nuclear reactors, and to improving the shelf life and effectiveness of drugs.

Other materials scientists work in the area of metallurgy, studying metal alloys and striving to improve their strength and other properties. Still others study how atoms and molecules attach to surfaces; their work feeds directly into the study of catalysts, and some materials scientists spend their lives designing new catalysts. They may design novel molecules with very specific shapes to catalyze specific industrial reactions; the catalysts they produce may be either organic or inorganic.

Since materials scientists are either physicists or chemists, they are paid on the same scales. Their job prospects, however, are somewhat better, for materials science is now a growing field, although research budgets are cramped. New techniques are available; there is a strong need for improved catalysts, and the electronics industry is straining for technological advances.

THE HOT SPOTS

At this writing one of the most exciting areas of research and development is that of high-temperature superconductors. It concerns physicists, chemists, and materials scientists, and it may before long offer benefits in more efficient power transmission, faster computers, and even quieter trains for all the rest of us. Superconductors carry electrical currents without resistance or loss, but until recently they were not practical for many uses because they had to be maintained at the temperature of liquid helium, very close to absolute zero; high-temperature superconductors work at the temperature of liquid nitrogen, which is much cheaper and easier to handle than liquid helium.

The physics of thermonuclear fusion and the chemistry of plasmas are also exciting areas, for a great deal of research and development effort is now going into the push for a fusion reactor. The hope is to have a prototype reactor before the end of this century and to be using thermonuclear fusion for a major part of the nation's energy supply by 2025.

Other energy areas also employ many chemists and physicists. The conversion of sunlight into electricity is already almost economic, and new methods promise the use of sunlight and catalysts to produce hydrogen (burnable as a fuel) from water. The finding, processing, and use of fossil fuels also employ many physical scientists; work on the physics and chemistry of combustion—in open flames and in engines—aims to reduce pollutant emissions. The nuclear industry employs physical scientists too, but that field may be fading now; nuclear power has lost much of the popularity it once enjoyed, and other alternatives seem more attractive.

Electronics and computers may be more exciting than any of the above, however, for the technology of both is growing at an awe-inspiring rate. It may not be long before a computer with the power of a human brain can rest in one's hand.

Even better than this, though, may be the areas of elementary particle physics and cosmology, the ultimately small and the ultimately large. The current models of particle accelerators—underground, circular tunnels miles in circumference—are revealing the finest structure of matter. The largest of them all, the Superconducting Super Collider (SSC), is now in the planning stages. When finished, the SSC will have a circumference of 53 miles; it may be in operation by the end of the century. The cosmologists are studying the beginning and the end of our universe and sketching theories that suggest the existence of many more universes besides our own. Many of their theories are based on the results of experiments in elementary particle physics. We will say a little more about the work of cosmologists in Chapter 8.

CAREERS ON CAMPUS

Like life and earth scientists, physical scientists teach and do research at universities and colleges, and teach without the research at community colleges. They may also teach high school students.

Thanks to past growth in faculty and to present and future declines in the population of students, the campus environment will not offer a great many jobs until the 1990s, when large numbers of faculty members are expected to retire. Competition will also be intense in research. In chemistry, as in the life sciences, many new doctorates will spend a year or two in the postdoctoral holding pattern.

CAREERS IN INDUSTRY

While most physicists work on campus, most chemists by far work in industry (see Table 15). They work in research and development and in production, in quality control and in marketing, and in many other positions. Physicists in industry occupy a similar range of jobs. Almost always, they serve the corporate goals of new products, productivity, efficiency, and profit. If they serve these goals well, physical scientists can easily wind up in managerial posts.

Table 15 Employment of doctorate physical scientists, 1985

	Educational institutions	Industry	Federal government
Chemists	16,073	24,067	1,831
Physicists/astronomers	13,627	6,214	2,453

Source: National Research Council

CAREERS IN GOVERNMENT

The federal government's physical scientists work for the departments of Energy, Defense, Interior, Justice, Commerce, Agriculture, and Health and Human Services, and for the National Bureau of Standards, National Institutes of Health, National Science Foundation, Smithsonian Institution, National Aeronautics and Space Administration, Environmental Protection Agency, Patent Office, Food and Drug Administration, and Occupational Safety and Health Administration. They are everywhere, as analysts, managers, administrators, inspectors, regulators, and congressional staffers. They are even lobbyists.

They are also, of course, researchers, and the physical sciences are the fields of "Big Science," of multimillion-dollar research projects. The life sciences have their big government research centers in the National Institutes of Health, the Centers for Disease Control, and the Department of Agriculture. A few big projects, such as the mapping of the human genome, are expected to cost $3 billion over a period of 10 to 15 years. The space sciences have missions to other planets, radio telescopes, and optical telescopes, all quite costly enough. But government research in the physical sciences, especially physics, dwarfs research in any other field. The national laboratories of Oak Ridge, Los Alamos, and Livermore-Berkeley work on nuclear physics, lasers, and thermonuclear fusion. The atom is probed by the particle accelerators of Brookhaven, New York; Batavia, Illinois; and others. The Superconducting Super Collider, to be located in Texas, will cost between $5 and $8 billion. Most "Big Science" projects are funded by the Departments of Energy and Defense.

ORGANIZATIONS FOR PHYSICAL SCIENTISTS

Physical scientists can belong to the American Association for the Advancement of Science, Sigma Xi, and more specialized societies. For prospective physicists, career information is available from the American Institute of Physics, 335 East 45 Street, New York, NY 10017. It offers the booklet *Physics: A Career for You?* Information about fields of physics can be obtained by writing, care of the AIP, to the following:

Society of Physics Students
American Physical Society
American Crystallographic Association
American Vacuum Society
Acoustical Society of America

More general information is available in the magazines *Physics Today* and *Bulletin of the Atomic Scientists.*

The big society for chemists is the American Chemical Society, 1155 16 Street NW, Washington, DC 20036. It offers a wealth of career information, runs an Employment Clearing House and an Employment Aids Office, and publishes the weekly *Chemical and Engineering News.* It also publishes *Student Affiliate Newsletter,* which contains much career information, and a variety of journals.

Other organizations of interest to prospective chemists include the Chemical Manufacturers Association (2501 M Street, Washington, DC 20037) and the American Institute of Chemical Engineers (345 East 47 Street, New York, NY 10017).

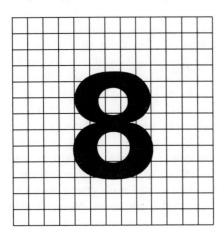

CAREERS IN THE SPACE SCIENCES

The Labor Department's *Occupational Outlook Handbook* lists only two space science careers: astronomer and aerospace engineer. We will consider the latter in Chapter 9, with all the other engineers. The former has its place in this chapter. But is it truly all alone? Is there really only one space science that is not a field of engineering?

Of course not. The space sciences are all those sciences and subfields that study or exploit some aspect of the space environment. Meteorologists are space scientists when they help design and launch, and then use, weather satellites and when they study the effects of solar activity on terrestrial weather. So are geographers when they design, launch, and use Earth-surveying satellites. So are geologists and geophysicists when they turn their eyes to other planets (as do *planetologists*) with the aid of flyby, orbiting, and landing spacecraft. So are life scientists when they focus on how space affects terrestrial organisms or on the prospects for extraterrestrial biology. So are chemists, metallurgists, biochemists, and others who wish to use the special qualities of the space environment (weightlessness, vacuum, etc.) in research and manufacturing.

The space sciences thus have something for scientists of every description. Yet space is not only for scientists. It is for all the human beings crowded together on this planet Earth, exposed to drought, flood, crop failures, and resource shortages. Relatively few will ever be able to leave this planet for others, or for the space habitats that may be built within the next century, but everyone can and will benefit from the virtually endless supplies of energy and raw materials available in space. We need only build the satellites that can trap the bountiful sunlight that shines 24 hours a day in orbit and convert it to electricity for use on Earth. We need only establish bases and mines on the moon and fetch home and process asteroids and comets. We need only move polluting industries into orbit. Earth's air and water will then be clean, and all Earth's billions will be able to enjoy a standard of living now known to too few.

This prescription sounds like science fiction. But serious plans for just such grandiose developments have been on the drawing boards for years, and the admittedly colossal expense is less of an obstacle than one might think. So far, we have used space mostly as a vantage point from which satellites can watch for storms, seek mineral deposits, provide cartographic data, appraise crops, and signal their positions to navigators on ships and planes. However, these simple uses of space have already repaid tenfold every dollar spent on space programs. There is no reason whatsoever to think that the benefit-to-cost ratio of further space programs will be any worse.

Yet this science fiction future will not come tomorrow. It is a long-term dream that, because the necessary initial investment is so large, depends on a thriving national and international economy. It also depends on the continued collection of information. What resources are available on the moon? We must spend more time there, prospecting from permanent bases. What resources are available in asteroids and comets? We must visit them and see. How safe is life in space? We must try it and see, with orbiting space stations, moon bases, and trips to the other planets of our solar system.

Other work of the space sciences also has its relevance to life on Earth. Solar and stellar physicists study how stars produce vast outpourings of energy from thermonuclear fusion reactions; they may provide the key to safe, cheap, workable fusion reactors on Earth. Planetologists—the geologists, geochemists, and geophysicists of space—study how other planets have formed and evolved; by giving us a base for comparison, they help us understand earthquakes, plate tectonics, volcanoes, and mineral deposits. Atmospheric scientists study the gaseous cloaks, clouds, and storms of other worlds; they help us understand the dynamics of earthly weather.

We have said that careers in science are dedicated to human survival. This may be nowhere truer than in the space sciences, for while these fields contribute to many human needs, they also offer an invaluable insurance policy. Life on a planet is vulnerable, for planets can be hit by massive bodies of rock such as the asteroid or comet that may have smashed into the Earth some 65 million years ago, extinguishing the dinosaurs and a myriad other life forms and marking the end of the Cretaceous period. That same disaster can happen again, as it has before. It is bound to, eventually. And the human species can have no protection as long as it remains confined to the surface of a single planet. On the other hand, if part of the species can move to space stations, space habitats, and other worlds, the species as a whole will be able to survive almost anything the universe can throw at it. Some humans will be able to sur-

vive asteroid impacts, ice ages, solar flares—even planetary thermonuclear war, Armageddon, the Götterdämmerung, of which we live in fear.

But first we must escape the naked surface of that round ball of rock
we call home. It is the space sciences that will help us do that. It is the
space sciences that will get our species off its planetary eight ball.

Sadly, it no longer seems likely that the U.S. will lead the way into
space, for the space program has lost an enormous amount of momen-
tum. The process began even as American astronauts were walking on
the moon, when then-President Nixon slashed the program's funds. The
program managed to continue, however, until it could launch the first re-
usable spacecraft, the space shuttle, and with it an enormous cargo of
hopes for the future. But then, in January 1986, the Space Shuttle *Challenger* exploded shortly after launch. Shortly after that, the nation lost
expendable rockets, and the spacecraft they were carrying, and virtually
the entire space program was suspended while the causes of the castas-
trophic failures were determined and solutions were sought. In 1988, an
explosion destroyed half of the U.S. capacity for manufacturing solid
rocket fuel, and it began to look as if the space program were doomed
forevermore. Although the shuttle was back in space by the end of 1988,
its future seems uncertain.

Meanwhile, the USSR and other nations have been launching satellites
and space probes without problem. The USSR now has its own space
shuttle. Has the U.S. lost the lead it once enjoyed in technical excellence?
Perhaps, though many think the problem is due more to the way politicians and professional managers have seized control of the space program from the technical experts. The U.S. must also cope with mounting
budget deficits which cut into all areas of federal funding.

ASTRONOMY

The oldest of the space sciences—and the only one we will treat purely
as a space science here—is astronomy. It is what may first leap to
mind when one thinks of "space science." In astronomy most of the
other space sciences find their origins. The builders of satellites and
spacecraft take places beside the builders of telescopes. Earth's weather
sidles up beside that of Jupiter and Mars and Venus. The work of geophysicists and planetologists, astrophysicists and plasma physicists, and
cosmologists and particle physicists all depends to some extent on
astronomy.

Traditionally, the astronomer has looked through telescopes to study
the stars—their movements, changes, types, and distributions—and the
planets and their satellites (moons). Today, very few astronomers actually apply eye to telescope. Modern astronomical equipment is electronic, controlled by computers, receiving the light of the stars and
planets with detectors far more efficient than either the human eye or

photographic film. Some telescopes observe the stars in wavelengths of light that the human eye cannot see at all. There are infrared telescopes, radio telescopes, and even ultraviolet, X-ray, and gamma ray telescopes (which work only in orbit, above the atmosphere). By the 1990s, the Hubble Space Telescope will be in orbit around the Earth; its human attendants and users will be hundreds of miles away, on the ground, and its unprecedentedly sharp images will be totally electronic.

Modern astronomers also exploit spacecraft. With the Mariner and Viking spacecraft, they have photographed the surface of Mars, and with the Vikings they have analyzed actual samples of the Martian surface. With the Pioneer and Voyager spacecraft, they have photographed the clouds and moons of Jupiter and the rings of Saturn and Uranus and gained reams of information to confound and delight the theorists. They have surveyed the fluxes of radiation, magnetic fields, and particles from Mercury to beyond Uranus. They have even probed the atmosphere and surface of Venus. And more.

With optical and radio telescopes, *solar astronomers* study the sun, its radiations, its magnetic fields, and its vast eruptions of plasma. With tanks of cleaning fluid deep in empty mines, they count neutrinos to study the processes of thermonuclear fusion that fuel the sun. With spacecraft, they sample and plot the solar wind, the flood of particles sleeting outward from the sun. They photograph and chart sunspots. They chase eclipses with aircraft to gain glimpses of the sun's corona.

Our sun is the nearest star, and solar astronomy is the close-at-hand subfield of *astrophysics*. Astrophysicists strive to understand how stars function and change as they age, how they form from clouds of dust and gas, and how they degenerate into white dwarfs, neutron stars, and black holes. They theorize about the unobservable and the yet unknown, trying to see through cryptic observations to the nature and characteristics of black holes and quasars.

Cosmologists probe the limits of the observable universe, over 10 billion light-years away from Earth; plot the distribution of galaxies and clusters of galaxies; and devise theories of how the universe, some 10 to 15 billion years ago, exploded from a pointlike mass. They are theorists, and they are kin to the particle physicists, who believe that at its beginning the universe was nothing but subatomic particles and energy. Some theorists suggest that our universe is but a bubble in some vaster cosmos that we can never know.

Very few of the nation's 3,000 or more astronomers ever spend more than a few weeks a year making observations with telescopes or other instruments. The rest of the time they spend teaching, writing and reading research proposals, keeping up with their field, attending scientific meetings, designing new observational instruments, and analyzing their own and others' observations. Many spend their time almost wholly on theories and mathematical models, working intimately with computers. Some are applied mathematicians, using computers and observations of the sun, moon, and planets to calculate tide tables and the orbits of both natural and artificial satellites.

Most jobs in astronomy require a doctorate in the field. Lesser degrees qualify one only for jobs as an assistant to a PhD astronomer, a data processor, an instrument builder or operator, or perhaps a writer or editor in the field. However, many of these jobs are filled by PhD astronomers. Competition for astronomical positions is keen, partly because the equipment necessary for observations—telescopes and spacecraft—is so expensive that it is in very limited supply and offers few people the chance to use it. Competition is also keen because the field is small and few replacements are needed, because the field is not growing at present and few new faculty are needed, and because more degrees are awarded in the field than there are positions available.

The job outlook may improve in the next few years if the Hubble Space Telescope reaches orbit and the space station now in the planning stages is built. If not, the field remains a fascinating one, and the pay is good. In 1983, federal astronomers and other space scientists averaged $46,000. Astronomers on campus make about the same as physicists.

THE HOT SPOTS

At the moment, federal funding for planetary exploration has fallen off drastically. For at least most of the next decade, space scientists will be restricted to analyzing moon rocks brought back to Earth by the old Apollo program; photographs and other data accumulated by past Viking, Pioneer, and Voyager spacecraft in their visits to Mars, Jupiter, Saturn, and Uranus; and other material from past trips past Mercury and Venus. New spacecraft data will probably be obtained when Voyager 2 passes Neptune. New expeditions to Venus and Jupiter are planned.

Far less mired in the budgetary swamp is the Hubble Space Telescope. Originally planned for launch in 1986, before the *Challenger* disaster set the shuttle program back, the orbiting telescope is now due to launch on a space shuttle in 1989. It will open the heavens as never before. Free of the atmosphere's fogs and turbulences, it will photograph the planets with a clarity so far achieved only by orbiting spacecraft. It will also provide vastly improved images of distant stars, and it may even be able to register the presence of other planetary systems.

X-ray, gamma ray, infrared, ultraviolet, and radio astronomy also offer the prospect of exciting discoveries, and a U.S. space station is now planned. Such a station, and the other projects it will enable and lead to, will give exciting employment to engineers, technicians, life scientists, physicists, chemists, and materials scientists. The space sciences may be in the doldrums now, but the future is wide open. It may even be open enough to warrant choosing a career in the space sciences in anticipation of a future explosion of space science activity.

CAREERS ON CAMPUS

Sixty percent of the nation's astronomers work for colleges, universities, or academically affiliated observatories, where they spend most of their time in teaching and research. One in five academic astronomers is a research associate, not faculty but staff; these jobs do not offer tenure and are supposedly short term, but some astronomers have held them for long periods. Postdoctoral positions also exist.

Science museums and planetariums employ a few astronomers blessed with a performer's flair for popularizing their field and reaching the public. The pay matches that of astronomers on campus, and many of the relatively few people in these jobs are very satisfied with their work.

CAREERS IN INDUSTRY

In the private sector, a few astronomers find work with scientific supply houses and astronomical magazines such as *Sky and Telescope*. More apply their training in computers, electronics, equipment design, and data analysis to nonastronomical research, for the astronomer's training is general enough and technical enough to open up many satisfying, challenging careers. Still more work for aerospace companies as spacecraft designers and operators, planners, and managers, or for companies that do space-related research on contract for government and other companies.

Non-astronomer space scientists work for satellite communications companies, energy companies, and companies that interpret and use the data produced by Earth resource surveying satellites. In the future, industry is likely to move into space more vigorously, pursuing resources on the moon and elsewhere, building solar power satellites and dwelling places, and setting up manufacturing facilities in orbit. For the present, however, most space science jobs lie on campus and with the government.

CAREERS IN GOVERNMENT

A very few space scientists—mostly ex-astronauts with degrees in astronomy, physics, and engineering—have become senators and representatives. But they are hardly representative of the 500 or so astronomers and other space scientists employed by the federal government in NASA or the Defense Department's U.S. Naval Observatory and U.S. Naval Research Laboratory. Some government astronomers are involved in maintaining and improving navigation systems, both with traditional ephemerides (tables and charts of moon, sun, and star positions) and with satellite beacons and tide tables. Some other space scientists work in meteorology and Earth resource surveying. Many astronomers and other space scientists work as researchers, planners, and managers in the space and defense programs.

The government's space activities are dominated by the Department of Defense and NASA. NASA's 1989 budget request came to $11.5 billion. By comparison, the portion of the Department of Defense's budget devoted to space science (planned for 1989) was slightly more than NASA's entire budget request, and included $5 billion for work on the Strategic Defense Initiative (SDI) alone. But this amount still represents only a piddling chunk of Defense's $300 billion total budget request for 1989.

NASA does not spend its money only on space, but also on aeronautics (see Table 16). The two fields often overlap, especially in the areas of engineering, navigation, and biological effects. The Defense Department's expenditures relate to weapons launch and guidance systems, intelligence gathering, and future manned satellites.

ORGANIZATIONS FOR SPACE SCIENTISTS

There is a wealth of organizations to which space scientists may belong, in addition to the multidisciplinary standbys (AAAS and Sigma Xi) and to many of the organizations for physical and earth scientists. The American Astronomical Society publishes several journals and a quarterly newsletter; for 35 cents it will send a booklet on careers in astronomy, which lists approved astronomy programs at colleges and universities across the country. It also runs a job service consisting of a monthly Job Register, a Candidates Register of résumés, and a Job Center at the society's meetings.

The American Institute of Aeronautics and Astronautics publishes books and journals (including one for students), runs employment workshops, and has career information available. The American Astronautical Society publishes books, a journal, and a newsletter; employment aid comes in the form of employer attendance at AAS meetings.

Among the many other organizations are the Aerospace Industries Association, the American Society for Aerospace Education, the International Astronautical Federation, and the Aerospace Medical Association. All are primarily for professionals in the space sciences, but amateurs who care about the space sciences and wish to encourage them may also join.

There are also many organizations that are primarily for amateurs and enthusiasts but count many professionals among their members. The most active of these groups is the National Space Society, one portion of which, the L-5 Society, was organized to encourage the building of space colonies and sworn not to disband until it can hold its final meeting on a space colony. It promotes a vigorous U.S. space program and public awareness of the importance of space development.

Table 16   NASA field installations

Ames Research Center, Moffett Field, California	Aircraft and spacecraft guidance and stability; space environmental physics; simulation methods; biomedical and biophysical research
Goddard Space Flight Center, Greenbelt, Maryland	Satellite development; astronomical research; Earth resources, weather, and communications; satellite tracking and data reception
Marshall Space Flight Center, Huntsville, Alabama	Spacecraft launch vehicle and support system R&D
Kennedy Space Center, Merritt Island, Florida	Primary U.S. launch facility
Langley Research Center, Hampton, Virginia	Aeronautics research; space structures and materials R&D
Johnson Space Center, Houston, Texas	Astronaut training; manned mission development; space technology R&D; Space Shuttle operations center
Lewis Research Center, Cleveland, Ohio	Advanced aircraft engine and spacecraft power plant and propulsion system R&D
National Space Technology Laboratories, Bay St. Louis, Mississippi	Spacecraft engine test firing; support for Space Shuttle main engine and main orbital propulsion system
Jet Propulsion Laboratory, Pasadena, California (operated under contract by California Institute of Technology)	Spacecraft tracking and data reception and processing; orbit computation and analysis R&D

Table 17   Societies and sources of further information for space scientists

Dr. Charles A. Tolbert
Education Officer
American Astronomical Society
Box 3818 University Station
Charlottesville, VA 22903

American Astronautical Society
6212-B Old Keene Mill Ct.
Springfield, VA 22152

American Institute of Aeronautics and Astronautics
1633 Broadway
New York, NY 10019

National Space Society
West Wing, Suite 203-W
600 Maryland Ave., S.W.
Washington, DC 20024

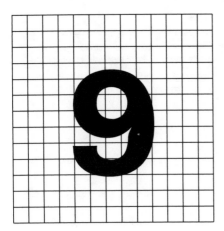

CAREERS IN ENGINEERING

The engineering "sciences" include architecture, surveying, aerospace, agricultural, automotive, biomedical, ceramic, chemical, civil, electrical and electronics, genetic, industrial, mechanical, metallurgical, mining, nuclear, and petroleum engineering. They are often close kin to the life, earth, physical, and space sciences. Their main difference is that the engineer is even more interested in specific, useful answers to problems than the applied researcher. Engineers are designers and builders of mechanical, electronic, and—most recently—biological devices. They plan factories to ease the task of production. They design and supervise mines to cope with local geological problems, find ore, and maintain safety. They seek the best ways to extract oil from the ground.

As a group, engineers are quite well paid. In 1986, industry paid new bachelor's graduates with no experience an average of $27,900. The top pay went to petroleum and chemical engineers. Civil engineers made the least, but even they averaged over $24,000 to start. New master's graduates averaged $33,100. New doctorates got $42,200.

The pay is so good and the demand for engineers is so high that few go on to obtain degrees beyond the bachelor's. This is partly because teaching jobs simply cannot compete with industrial pay scales. New bachelor's graduates often see little reason to grind away at a higher degree when they can begin enjoying high pay immediately. The result is a shortage of teachers.

Estimates vary, but according to the National Science Foundation, there were a total of 1,921,000 engineers in 1984. Of this number, 1,672,000 worked for industry, 82,000 worked in education, and 167,000 worked for the federal government. According to the Bureau of Labor Statistics, in 1986 there were only 1,371,000 engineers, of which 40,000 worked on campus and 184,000 worked for federal, state, and local gov-

Figure 5 Engineering employment (000s), 1986

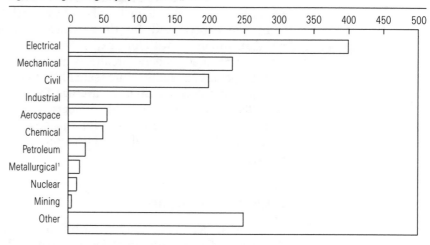

¹Includes ceramic and materials engineers.

Source: Bureau of Labor Statistics

ernments (over half of these public-sector engineers worked for the federal Departments of Defense, Energy, Transportation, Agriculture, and Interior, and for the National Aeronautics and Space Administration). Over half of all engineers worked for manufacturing industries; 470,000 jobs were in nonmanufacturing industries.

ARCHITECTURE

Architects are both artists and applied physicists and materials scientists. They design and supervise the construction of buildings—houses, factories, offices, skyscrapers, airport terminals, hotels, and more. They strive to make their products attractive, usable, energy-efficient, sturdy, safe, and economical. They must thus know the strengths, durabilities, and costs of materials; be able to plan how materials will go together and interact; and be able to calculate loads and stresses on each element of a structure. They must also take into account building codes, zoning laws, access laws, and other regulations, and they need skills in drawing and managing.

In 1986, there were 84,000 active architects in this country. All had licenses obtained by passing state exams. To qualify to take the exams, they had earned a bachelor's degree in architecture and gained three years of experience working for a licensed architect.

In some cases, experience replaced the bachelor's degree. Most of the nation's 93 accredited architecture programs offer a five-year bachelor's program or a six-year master's program. There are also two-year community college architecture programs that prepare students to transfer into the professional schools or to take jobs as architectural drafters.

In 1986, experienced, full-time architects averaged more than $30,000 per year. Architects with long experience and good reputations made upwards of $50,000. Federal architects averaged $36,500.

Job openings in architecture seem likely to be in good supply, with employment rising faster than the average for all occupations through the year 2000. However, the number of degrees earned will rise too, and there will be competition, especially for the best jobs. In addition, the job prospects in the field will depend closely on the state of the national economy.

LANDSCAPE ARCHITECTURE

Where architects design and build buildings, landscape architects work with space. Given a site, they decide where buildings, roads, parks, and lawns will go. They are planners and artists, and the knowledge they exploit is of wind, sun, rain, drainage, and plant biology. They may also supervise construction and work with architects.

The nation's 18,000 landscape architects enjoy an optimistic job outlook, for their field grows with concern for the environment and for urban and regional planning. Most have a four- or five-year bachelor's degree in landscape architecture, and in many states they must be licensed. Beginners average about $18,000 a year. With experience, they move into the $25,000–50,000 range. Those who work for the federal government can expect a little more. The government pays new bachelor's graduates up to $18,400 and graduates with higher degrees up to $22,500. Federal landscape architects averaged $36,600 in 1986.

SURVEYING

Surveyors are measurers of land. With theodolites, transits, and laser instruments, and even satellites and radio telescopes, they measure elevations, distances, contours, angles, and directions. They mark the boundaries of house lots and subdivisions and the routes of new roads, keep tunnels on course and level, and monitor the land surface for bulges that may promise earthquakes and volcanic eruptions. They also record their measurements with maps, sketches, and reports. They are essential to cartography, construction projects, land valuation, and the preparation of legal deeds. Extreme accuracy is their watchword.

In 1986, there were about 94,000 surveyors in the United States. Some held bachelor's degrees in surveying. Many were graduates of one-, two-, or three-year programs offered by community colleges. The bachelor's degree is most essential for specialized surveyors such as *photogramme-trists,* who work from aerial and satellite photos. Other specialists include *land, marine, geodetic,* and *geophysical prospecting surveyors* and *mosaicists* and *map editors.*

In 1987, the federal government paid high school graduates with little or no experience less than $11,000. Federal pay goes up about $1,000 with every year of post–high school education, and federal surveying technicians average about $18,200 per year. Land surveyors start at annual salaries of $14,822 or $18,358 and average about $30,000. Specialized surveyors may make more. Surveyors employed by industry enjoy comparable earnings.

Employment of surveyors should grow about as fast as the average for all occupations through the year 2000, but since much of the present and future demand is related to construction, the job outlook is by no means certain. If the economy strengthens, construction will increase and more surveyors will be needed. If the economy fails to strengthen, construction will decline and many new surveying graduates may fail to find jobs in this field.

AEROSPACE ENGINEERING

The American Institute of Aeronautics and Astronautics says that "aerospace engineering and technology is probably the most specialized and yet the most diversified field there is." Aerospace engineers design and build aircraft and spacecraft, satellites, rocket engines, guidance systems, nose cones, and more. They deal with the physics of propulsion, fluid mechanics and aerodynamics, thermodynamics, structures, flight and space mechanics, and energy. Outside the aerospace field, they apply their knowledge to energy conservation, to the design of an artificial heart, to evaluation of the wind loads on a skyscraper, or to the designing of an efficient wind turbine.

Aerospace engineers work on the analysis of problems and data, the design of aerospace devices, materials and product testing, manufacturing, servicing, marketing, and management. Some work more as scientists than as engineers, doing research and development work for industry or government or teaching and researching on campus.

There were about 53,000 U.S. aerospace engineers in 1986, two-thirds of them working in the aerospace industry. Many had no more than bachelor's degrees; master's degrees and doctorates are essential for academic teaching and research and for promotion to senior research and management positions. Employment in the field will grow faster than average if the defense budget continues to increase and if the space program successfully revives.

AGRICULTURAL ENGINEERING

Agricultural engineers work on the design, construction, testing, selling, and servicing of equipment for preparing soil and planting, cultivating, harvesting, and processing crops. They also design buildings and equipment for animal care and processing, storage systems, greenhouses, power supplies, control systems, and water supplies. They may work in irrigation, flood control, land reclamation, waste treatment and disposal, soil and water conservation, and land use. They may even work on recreation facilities.

There is and will be strong demand for agricultural engineers, and the pay is well above average. Most workers in the field need only bachelor's degrees; higher degrees are needed only for research and teaching on campus.

AUTOMOTIVE ENGINEERING

Automotive engineers do not work only with automobiles. They design, develop, test, and build vehicles of all kinds, including cars, trucks, motorcycles, aircraft and spacecraft, and industrial machinery. They work with engines, fuels, lubricants, electrical systems, electronics, structures, hydraulics, materials, and safety systems. The field, in fact, includes engineers of many kinds.

Demand is strong and the pay is good. Graduate degrees are essential only for academic positions and for senior research and management positions.

BIOMEDICAL ENGINEERING

Biomedical engineers include engineers of all kinds—aerospace, automotive, ceramic, electrical, mechanical—who are interested in medical problems. They design and build medical diagnostic and treatment instruments, prostheses, artificial organs, and pacemakers. They develop medical uses for new technologies such as lasers. They adapt computers to the needs of medical data processing and modernize laboratory, hospital, and clinic structures and procedures.

Bioengineers, biotechnologists, or bioenvironmental engineers specialize in less medical areas. They work on maintaining and improving environmental quality and protecting plants, animals, and humans from toxic substances and pollutants. *Medical engineers* specialize in medical diagnosis and therapy, developing instruments, materials, devices, computer systems, and artificial organs. *Clinical engineers* concentrate on improving health care delivery systems.

Most biomedical engineers have a bachelor's degree in an engineering area and a master's or doctorate in biomedical engineering, but bachelor's degrees in biomedical engineering are becoming available. The pay is good, and though there are not a great number of job openings in the field, since relatively few people earn degrees in biomedical engineering, competition for the available openings may not prove too intense. Biomedical engineers with advanced degrees will have little trouble finding jobs, especially in teaching and research.

CERAMIC ENGINEERING

Ceramic engineers work with nonmetallic, inorganic materials—ceramics. They match known ceramic materials to new uses, develop new ceramics, and devise the machinery for manufacturing them. As researchers, they may seek new ceramics with specific properties and new production processes with lower costs.

Most of the nation's ceramic engineers work in the stone, clay, and glass industries. They may specialize in heat-resistant materials, pottery, insulators, brick and tile, electronic materials, metal coatings, glass, abrasives, or cement. They may also work in the nuclear industry, since uranium oxide ceramics provide the fuel elements of nuclear reactors.

To become a ceramic engineer calls for a bachelor's degree. Higher degrees are necessary only for research and teaching on campus. The job outlook for the next few years is good, with many job openings in nuclear energy, defense, electronics, medical science, pollution control, and energy handling.

CHEMICAL ENGINEERING

Chemical engineers turn chemistry into products. In research and development, they devise economical and efficient production processes. They then design, construct, and operate equipment and factories that use those processes. Some chemical engineers teach and do research on campus, while about a third of the 52,000 chemical engineers in the country are managers and supervisors.

Most chemical engineers, like most chemists, work for industry. There they work with pharmaceuticals, cosmetics, paints, dyes, pesticides, fertilizers, and other chemical products. They may also work on petroleum refining; the purification of polluted water and air; pollution prevention; waste management; the recycling of metals, glass, and plastics; and the development of solar and geothermal energy. In every case, they need a talent for problem-solving and skill with computers.

The usual preparation for a career in chemical engineering involves a four- or five-year bachelor of science in the field. Higher degrees are essential for careers on campus and helpful for senior research and management positions in industry and government, but the American Chemical Society does call them optional. A bachelor-level chemical engineer could start at about $29,000 in 1986; a new master's, at $35,000; and a new doctorate, at $44,000. In all cases, chemical engineers earn several thousand dollars more a year than chemists.

Despite the dependence of industry on chemical engineers, job openings in the field are expected to grow no faster than the average for all occupations through the year 2000. Much of the growth will be in pharmaceutical, biotechnological, and nonmanufacturing industries.

CIVIL ENGINEERING

Often working closely with other engineers and architects, civil engineers design and oversee the construction of buildings, roads and highways, railways, airports, tunnels, bridges, and water supply and sewage systems. Their specialties include soil mechanics and structural, hydraulic, environmental or sanitary, transportation, and highway engineering. Many of the nation's 199,000 civil engineers are supervisors or managers. Most work for federal, state, and local governments or for the construction industry.

A bachelor's degree is essential for a career in civil engineering, but a master's degree is becoming more and more necessary for continued, effective functioning. The employment outlook is quite favorable, for the U.S. population is still growing (albeit slowly), and the next few years will call for a fair amount of design and construction of new manufacturing plants, defense installations, transportation systems, and energy facilities.

ELECTRICAL AND ELECTRONICS ENGINEERING

The best way to describe the breadth of electrical and electronics engineering may be to list the 31 technical societies of the Institute of Electrical and Electronics Engineers (IEEE):

Acoustics, speech and signal processing
Aerospace and electronic systems
Antennas and propagation
Broadcast, cable and consumer electronics
Circuits and systems
Communications
Components, hybrids and manufacturing technology
Computers
Control systems
Education
Electrical insulation
Electromagnetic compatibility
Electron devices
Engineering management
Engineering in medicine and biology
Geoscience and remote sensing
Industrial electronics
Industry applications
Information theory

Instrumentation and measurement

Magnetics

Microwave theory and techniques

Nuclear and plasma sciences

Power engineering

Professional communications

Quantum electronics and applications

Reliability

Social implications of technology

Sonics and ultrasonics

Systems, man and cybernetics

Vehicular technology

It is a diverse field. Electrical and electronics engineers find work wherever electrical and electronic equipment are used and wherever electrical and electronic phenomena arise. They develop new products, test and maintain equipment, solve operating problems, and manage projects. Many are involved in selling.

Most of the nation's 401,000 electrical and electronics engineers have bachelor's degrees. Higher degrees are in most demand on campus and in senior management. The job outlook is better than average thanks to the current boom in computer and communications technology. Many of the best jobs are in the computer industry, and employers there compete fiercely for the best workers. A new bachelor's graduate can easily start at over $28,000 a year, and even at over $40,000.

GENETIC ENGINEERING

Genetic engineers are molecular biologists and geneticists who work on ways to transplant genes from one living thing to another. So far, they have produced bacteria that manufacture human proteins for use in medicine; the proteins include interferon and a number of hormones and vaccines. They have also produced a bacterium that does not serve as a nucleus for ice crystal formation, which, spread on fields, could decrease the likelihood of frost damage to crops. In addition, they have begun to transplant disease resistance genes into crop plants. Future products may include plants that need no fertilizer, higher-yielding crop plants, more efficient meat animals, and ways to replace the defective genes responsible for hereditary diseases.

No one knows how many genetic engineers there are, for this field of engineering is as yet too young to be classified as an occupation by the Department of Labor. However, we can say that a doctorate seems to be essential for work in the field, that the pay is generous, and that the job prospects are limited only by the future success of the field. A few companies formed to commercialize the technology of genetic engineering, such as Genentech, have thrived and their R&D budgets have expanded tremendously. Other companies have been much less successful.

INDUSTRIAL ENGINEERING

In 1986, this nation employed about 117,000 industrial engineers, mostly in the manufacturing industries, but also in insurance companies, banks, construction and mining firms, utilities, and hospitals. Some industrial engineers work in government as regulators and inspectors, and some work on campus.

Industrial engineers focus on how best to coordinate people, machines, and materials. They design production lines, do long-range planning, and work on computerized information systems, among other things. Many wind up in management, and advancement is typically rapid.

The related *manufacturing engineers* concentrate on manufacturing processes. They devise new methods and specify the details of standard methods for new products. They also design and set up manufacturing equipment, and they are essential to efficient production.

Industrial engineers can expect pay almost as good as that of electrical engineers. Only a bachelor's degree in the field is necessary for most jobs. Higher degrees aid, but are not essential to, promotion; they are necessary only on campus. Employment should grow more rapidly than the average for all occupations through the year 2000.

MECHANICAL ENGINEERING

Some mechanical engineers are industrial, biomedical, automotive, agricultural, or aerospace engineers. Their concerns are mechanical devices of various kinds, from can openers to automobile transmissions and engines to rocket fuel pumps. They work in the conversion of energy from natural sources—solar, wind, water, geothermal, coal, oil, nuclear—to useful forms. They design and develop machines that provide and use power. Many work in the transportation, electric utility, heating, and cooling industries.

Mechanical engineers may specialize in the needs of a particular industry, such as the paper, textile, construction, or petroleum industry, or in motor vehicles; marine equipment; energy conversion systems; heating, ventilating, and air conditioning systems; or instrumentation.

Many mechanical engineers work in the design and development of new devices. Others work in maintenance, production, sales, and management. Some teach on campus. All are professional problem solvers: given a need, they can either design a solution or point to the necessary device.

There were 233,000 mechanical engineers in the United States in 1986. About three-quarters of them worked in the manufacturing industries.

Most had four- or five-year bachelor's degrees in the field. Some had higher degrees. The job outlook is better than average for the next few years, partly because of the growing complexity of industrial processes. The pay runs a little worse than that for electrical engineers, with bachelor's mechanical engineers averaging $27,864 to start in 1986.

METALLURGICAL ENGINEERING

The metallurgical engineer deals with ores, the extraction of metals from them, and the refining, alloying, casting, fabricating, and heat treating of the metals. In research, he or she strives to develop better methods of doing all these things, sometimes even coming up with biological techniques such as the use of acid-secreting bacteria to leach metal compounds from copper and uranium ores. Metallurgical engineers also design, develop, and operate plants and equipment for their field.

Metallurgical engineers may specialize in *physical metallurgy,* the study and analysis of the properties of metals; in *process engineering,* plant design and processing techniques; and in *materials science,* the study of the properties and uses of metals and nonmetallic materials (including ceramics and plastics). Metallurgical engineers are crucial to transportation, communications, and energy systems, and because metal processing—especially the smelting of metals from ores—contributes so much to industrial pollution, they are often deeply involved with society's concern for the environment.

One-fifth of the nation's 18,000 metallurgical, ceramic, and materials engineers work in the metal-working industries. More work for companies that make machinery, electrical equipment, and vehicles. Some work for government and on campus. All enjoy a better than average job outlook, with an average starting pay of $27,864 in 1986. A bachelor's degree is enough to enter the field. Metallurgical engineers with higher degrees find employment in research and on campus.

MINING ENGINEERING

Mining engineers operate somewhere in between the fields of geologists and metallurgical engineers. One specialty, in fact, is that of the *mining geologist,* who seeks new sources of minerals. *Mining engineers* are in charge of extracting the minerals once they are discovered. They design and supervise the construction of open-pit and underground mines, oversee the construction of ore transportation systems and living facilities for the miners, and are responsible for safe ventilation, power and water supplies, communications, and maintenance. *Mineral processing engineers* direct the separation of minerals from their ore by crushing, grinding, and chemical treatment. Their degrees are actually in metallurgical engineering, and they may develop new techniques or equipment.

Mining engineers often specialize in a particular mineral. There are thus such specialties as *coal mining engineers, copper mining engineers,* and *uranium mining engineers.* In each case, the engineer faces special problems of extraction, safety, and environmental protection. The last often includes restoring a worked-out mine to a condition approximating that of the land before the mine was opened.

In 1986, there were about 5,200 mining engineers in this country, each with a bachelor's degree in his or her field. Those with higher degrees find work in research and on campus. Most mining engineers work for mining companies or manufacturers of mining equipment. The job outlook is poor, for employment is expected to stay about the same through the year 2000. The reason is that the demand for coal, metal, and other minerals is not expected to grow very much. In the long run, however, prices for these commodities will increase, mining activity will accelerate, and employment prospects are bound to improve.

NUCLEAR ENGINEERING

Nuclear engineers are mechanical engineers who specialize in the design, construction, and operation of nuclear power plants on land and at sea. They may also do research, work on nuclear fuels, design and build nuclear weapons, and find industrial and medical uses for radioactive materials. Safety is often their main concern; in nuclear power plants, they must be able to respond immediately and correctly to any of a wide range of problems. When they fail, the consequences may include exposure of thousands of people to life-threatening radiation, as happened in the Chernobyl disaster in Russia.

There were about 14,000 nuclear engineers in the U.S. in 1986. About a fifth worked for the federal government. In private industry, the starting pay for new bachelor's graduates averages $27,696 per year. Employment is not expected to change through the year 2000, largely because few nuclear power plants are being built, due both to public fears of nuclear power and to less than expected demand for electricity.

PETROLEUM ENGINEERING

Petroleum engineers are essentially mining engineers who deal with oil and gas. They explore and drill for these fossil fuels, striving to maximize their recovery by such tactics as injecting steam, detergents, and water into wells to force out the oil and gas. At present, oil companies can recover only about half of the oil or gas in a deposit tapped by a well. With shortages looming and fuel prices high, petroleum engineers thus spend much of their time trying to increase recovery rates. In addition, they do research on and supervise well drilling on land and at sea.

There were about 22,000 petroleum engineers in 1986. Most worked in the petroleum industry. Some worked for federal and state governments and on campus. Most had bachelor's degrees; those with higher degrees worked in research and on campus.

The job outlook is expected to grow more slowly than the average for all occupations through the year 2000, unless the price of oil rises significantly. In time, many new jobs will involve new sources of oil, such as oil shale, and the application of petroleum engineering techniques to other areas such as drilling wells to tap geothermal energy. The average starting pay is higher than that for any other engineering specialty, being $33,000 in 1986.

TECHNICIANS AND TECHNOLOGISTS

Like the life, earth, physical, and space sciences, engineering provides jobs for numerous technicians. In 1986, in fact, all fields of engineering together employed some 689,000 technicians, 40 percent of them in manufacturing. The jobs of technicians are more limited in scope than those of engineers or scientists; they require less training; and they carry less pay. The training frequently consists of a two-year community college or technical institute program. Training can also come on the job or in the military.

In 1986, full-time engineering technicians averaged almost $25,000 per year. Federal engineering technicians started at $11,802, $13,248, or $14,822, depending on education and experience. The job prospects are excellent across the board.

The engineering technician's work may lie in any area of technology—aeronautical engineering; air conditioning, heating, and refrigeration; civil engineering; biomedical engineering; electronics; chemical engineering; manufacturing; industrial engineering; mechanical engineering; instrumentation; and more. The work generally consists of operating equipment and instruments, making measurements, doing calculation, and otherwise following the instructions of a supervising engineer. Engineering technicians may also work in sales, technical writing, or maintenance, or as service representatives. The pay for chemical engineering technicians is rather higher than that for others, running several thousand dollars less than the pay for BS chemists.

The Labor Department counts separately 348,000 *drafters,* who prepare engineering and architectural drawings and blueprints. Their pay is comparable to that of technicians, and the necessary education is the same—employers actually prefer drafters who have technical training. The job prospects are best for those with two-year degrees in drafting and with training or experience with computer-aided drafting systems, a development that is displacing many lower-level drafters.

Somewhat above the level of the technician, yet still below the level of the engineer, is the *engineering technologist.* Where the engineer designs, plans, constructs, operates, and maintains complete technical devices and systems, the technologist solves technical problems, organizing people, materials, and equipment to design, operate, maintain, and manage technical engineering projects. At least, so says the Engineer's Council for Professional Development. It seems clear that the engineering technologist must do many of the same things as engineers, albeit with a somewhat more practical emphasis. As a field, engineering technology is too new to appear in the Labor Department's *Occupational Outlook Handbook*. It exists, for it is mentioned in the career brochures of many engineering societies and students can earn four-year bachelor's degrees in it, but it is apparently still splitting away from engineering as the latter has been defined. Many people become technologists by transferring into a four-year program after completing a two-year degree as an engineering technician.

THE HOT SPOTS

The most exciting careers for the future may lie in aerospace engineering. It will be aerospace engineers who develop and build the technology of the true space age on whose brink we sit. The future may hold space stations, solar power satellites, lunar and asteroid mining, manned expeditions to Mars and other planets, vast telecommunications platforms, and other marvels. Many aerospace engineers will live and work in space; they may even be among the first colonists of other worlds. They will bring home to Earth badly needed information, energy, and raw materials. They will enrich the human species, and they may even win credit for preserving it from the poverty that must follow the exhaustion of terrestrial resources.

If the space age blooms as it should, it will offer new opportunities to engineers of all kinds. Whether it blooms or not, electrical and electronic engineers will find a vigorous future in the booming technology of information handling—computers and communications. Biomedical and genetic engineering will flourish. Chemical engineers will remain in great demand, as will petroleum and mining engineers.

According to the Bureau of Labor Statistics of the U.S. Department of Labor, engineering as a single field can expect to see a 32 percent (444,000 jobs) growth in employment from 1986 to 2000. The five subfields of engineering that can expect the greatest percentage growth are civil engineering (25%), electrical and electronics engineering (48%), industrial engineering (30%), mechanical engineering (33%), and metallurgical, ceramic, and materials engineering (25%). In addition, architects can expect 30 percent growth in employment, and landscape architects 38 percent. Numerically, the lead settles on civil engineering (50,000 jobs), electrical and electronics engineers (192,000), industrial engineers (35,000), and mechanical engineers (76,000). Note that electrical and electronics engineering accounts for almost half of the growth in engineering employment.

CAREERS ON CAMPUS

Of the nation's 1,371,000 (BLS estimate) engineers of all kinds, less than three percent work on campus, and there is constant concern that not enough young engineers are pursuing doctorates in their fields with an eye on academic careers. Industrial pay scales are too tempting. Relatively few students are willing to stay in school, struggling to win a degree that will qualify them for research and teaching at less pay than they can earn in industry with just a bachelor's degree. Doctoral-level engineers on campus averaged $42,500 in 1983, considerably less than the $49,900 they could expect in industry.

Some young engineers do choose an academic career. They prefer the work environment on campus, or they are dedicated to teaching. They also enjoy the opportunity to supplement their income with a variety of consulting jobs. Nevertheless, the nation's colleges and universities are concerned that too few are entering academic careers to ensure an adequate supply of trained engineers for the future. Some schools are thus raising pay for their engineering faculty, or seeking funds from state and federal governments and from industry to do so. Engineering careers on campus are thus becoming more competitive with industrial careers.

We should note that a number of museums of science and technology employ engineers in the preparation of exhibits and in related research. Campus-affiliated research centers such as the Jet Propulsion Laboratory in Pasadena, California, also employ engineers.

CAREERS IN INDUSTRY

Most engineers work in industry and enjoy high pay. Some do applied research. Most are involved with manufacturing, construction, production, and planning. Many work in management, sales, maintenance, technical writing, and other areas.

CAREERS IN GOVERNMENT

Almost 14 percent of all engineers are employed by federal, state, and local government. They work in federal planning and construction programs, state highway departments, and municipal public service departments. The federal government uses engineers in the military, perhaps especially in the Army Corps of Engineers, and elsewhere in the Defense Department. The Departments of Energy, Agriculture, Transportation, and Interior also employ engineers, as does NASA. Some federal engineers are industrial safety inspectors; energy regulators; congressional staffers, advisers, and fellows; and even astronauts.

In 1986, the federal government paid experienced engineers an average of $38,000. BS engineers could start at $18,710 or $23,170 (depending on their college grades), a pay scale quite comparable to that of industry.

A new master's graduate could start at $25,980, and a new doctorate could get $28,039.

ORGANIZATIONS FOR ENGINEERS

Table 18 lists a number of organizations for engineers. There are a few all-inclusive societies, such as the Accreditation Board of Engineering and Technology and the National Society of Professional Engineers, both of which offer a variety of career-related publications and will supply a price list on request. Both have available lists of schools whose engineering programs are approved.

In addition, every engineering specialty has its own professional society. Most of these societies supply career pamphlets on request. Some supply help to young engineers seeking jobs. All hold periodic meetings at which the members deliver papers, socialize, and make contacts that may lead to future job offers. Employers also attend these meetings, often with the aim of recruiting employees.

It is worth noting that very few engineers belong to minority groups. In 1972, only 1,300 of 43,000 engineering graduates were black, Hispanic, or native American. Since then, the National Action Council for Minorities in Engineering (NACME) has used corporate and foundation funds to supply scholarships for minority engineering students. By 1984, blacks alone accounted for 2,000 engineering graduates, and the numbers of minority engineers are growing. For up-to-date contact information, write, enclosing a self-addressed, stamped envelope, to the National Engineering Council for Guidance (see Table 18); the NECG also distributes information for many other engineering societies, including the Society of Women Engineers.

Table 18 Societies and sources of further information for engineers

Accreditation Board for Engineering and Technology, Publications Office

American Institute of Chemical Engineers

American Society of Civil Engineers

American Society of Mechanical Engineers
345 East 47 Street
New York, NY 10017

National Institute of Ceramic Engineers
757 Brooks Edge Plaza Dr.
Westerville, OH 43081

American Chemical Society
1155 16 Street NW
Washington, DC 20036

American Institute of Industrial Engineers, Inc.
25 Technology Park/Atlanta
Norcross, GA 30092

Table 18 (continued)

Society of Manufacturing Engineers
P.O. Box 930, One SME Dr.
Dearborn, MI 48121

Society of Automotive Engineers
400 Commonwealth Drive
Warrendale, PA 15096

National Society of Professional Engineers
1420 King St.
Alexandria, VA 22314

American Institute of Architects
1735 New York Avenue NW
Washington, DC 20006

National Engineering Council for Guidance
1420 King Street, Suite 405
Alexandria, VA 22314

Institute of Electrical and Electronics Engineers, Inc.
United States Activities Board
1111 19th Street NW, Suite 608
Washington, DC 20036

The Metallurgical Society of AIME
420 Commonwealth Dr.
Warrendale, PA 15086

The Society of Mining Engineers of AIME
Caller Number D
Littleton, CO 80137

Society of Petroleum Engineers
PO Box 833836
Richardson, TX 75083

American Society of Landscape Architects
1733 Connecticut Avenue NW
Washington, DC 20009

American Congress on Surveying and Mapping
210 Little Falls Street
Falls Church, VA 22046

American Society for Photogrammetry and Remote Sensing
210 Little Falls Street
Falls Church, VA 22046

American Institute of Aeronautics and Astronautics, Inc.
AIAA Student Programs
The Aerospace Center
370 L'Enfant Plaza
Washington, DC 20024

American Society of Agricultural Engineers
2950 Niles Road
St. Joseph, MI 49085

Biomedical Engineering Society
P.O. Box 2399
Culver City, CA 90231

Alliance for Engineering in Medicine and Biology
1101 Connecticut Ave., NW, Suite 700
Washington, DC 20036

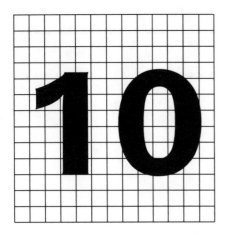

CAREERS IN MATHEMATICS AND COMPUTER SCIENCE

Mathematics is in some ways a peculiar field. For all its dedication to preciseness and system, for all its production of equations and graphs, it is not quite a science. It cannot be, for it cannot use the scientific method, at least in the usual sense. A mathematician cannot make observations or perform experiments. He or she cannot build theories.

What, then, is mathematics? It is the study and exploitation of the intrinsic properties of numbers. It is also the invention and exploration of rules of relationship and the manipulation of symbols (which may or may not refer to numbers). It approaches science most closely as a *tool* of science when it deals with actual phenomena, in measurement, calculation, and statistics. Otherwise, it is far more an art, its product flowing according to definite and often elaborate rules from the mind of the mathematician.

The distinction between mathematics as science and mathematics as art is neither arbitrary nor artificial. "Pure" mathematicians, like basic researchers in other fields, guide their work solely according to the dictates of curiosity. In fact, they often pride themselves on the irrelevance of their work to the real world. They build abstract algebras—systems of rules and relations—and explore the properties of numbers, interconnected lines ("graphs" and "knots"), and algebraic equations. Happily, their work often finds applications in physics, chemistry, cartography, and other fields. Oddly, some pure mathematicians seem to feel offended when their beautifully useless constructions turn out to be useful after all.

"Applied" mathematicians are more interested in the uses of math. They use their knowledge of differential equations, calculus, algebra, probability, and so on to solve problems in economics, biology, engineering, physics, and other fields. They observe a scientific or technical problem, hypothesize a mathematical approach to the problem, and experiment to see whether the approach works. They thus use a form of the scientific method, and they are much more scientists in the sense we are most familiar with. Pure mathematicians are much more like artists in their motivations and in the way their work flows from within themselves rather than from without.

Like other scientists, applied mathematicians have to live with the unattainability of ultimate truth. Only their observations—the problems they face and the data they work with—are facts. Their solutions may work, but they may also be open to improvement. Pure mathematicians, on the other hand, do know truth. If they make no errors, then the logical edifices they construct from a handful of rules are immune to argument or improvement. They can only be extended.

Upper-level careers in research and teaching are available in pure and applied mathematics. At lower levels, mathematicians are accountants, actuaries, bookkeepers, and statisticians. When they become more interested in the machinery of computation than in the process or results, they enter the computer sciences as designers, operators, programmers, and service technicians.

MATHEMATICS

Sixty percent (29,000) of all mathematicians work on campus, teaching and doing pure and applied research. The remaining 20,000 work in the communications, chemical, aerospace, computer, and data processing industries, and for the federal government, especially the Department of Defense and NASA.

Almost all pure mathematicians are employed by colleges and universities, largely because their research is not immediately useful to industry and government. They must generally have a doctorate in their field, and they earn pay comparable to that of other faculty members.

Applied mathematicians find jobs in a greater variety of places, and they can go to work after obtaining a bachelor's, a master's, or a doctoral degree. New bachelor's graduates started in 1986 at an average salary of $24,400; with the federal government, the 1987 figure for bachelor's graduates was $14,800 or $18,400 (depending on grades). New master's graduates averaged $30,600; the federal government paid $22,500 or $27,200 in 1987. New doctorates made $39,500, getting $27,200 or $32,600 from the federal government in 1987. Federal mathematicians with experience averaged over $38,000.

The work of the applied mathematician can involve constructing models to forecast sales; allocating services and resources in a firm or a political unit; calculating the strength, safety, and cost of designs for buildings and machines; studying chemical reactions; and simulating complex devices such as nuclear reactors and spacecraft. The actual process of work involves:

Defining a problem or question.

Breaking the problem into components and verbally describing their relationships.

Refining the descriptions of components and relationships in mathematical terms, using equations, inequalities, variables, and other devices. This amounts to constructing a mathematical model, either on paper or as a computer model or simulation.

Pulling together the data necessary to plug numbers into the model's equations and checking to see that the model accurately reflects the original problem.

Solving the model's equations.

Evaluating and interpreting the results in order to make the limits of their applicability clear and explain how to use the results.

Mathematicians with bachelor's degrees may solve many problems themselves. Perhaps more often, they are involved in managing large data collections; computing statistics; designing, operating, and programming computers; and teaching high school. They may become actuaries (see below).

Mathematicians with master's degrees may teach in community colleges and some four-year schools. In industry and government, they may be part of research and problem-solving teams in engineering, physics, chemistry, and forecasting.

Mathematicians with doctorates can teach at colleges and universities, do original research, and lead research and problem-solving teams. They may also become independent consultants.

Because most mathematicians work on campus, the job outlook is not as bright as it is in some other fields. The Department of Labor expects employment to grow about as fast as the average for all occupations through the year 2000. The best opportunities will be for those with doctorates. More jobs will exist in industry and government than on campus, especially in areas related to computers. The best use of a bachelor's degree in mathematics may be as preparation for graduate work in another science.

STATISTICS

Statisticians are specialists in probability. They analyze data and report on the odds that an average, say, is a true measurement of some quantity and not a chance peculiarity of the data collection process. They develop new tests for the significance of data and apply old tests. They apply their knowledge to the design of psychological and achievement tests; the calculation of insurance premiums; the analysis and design of breeding experiments in agriculture and laboratory genetics; the calculation of the odds that a child will have a birth defect; market analysis and forecasting; weather forecasting; economics; drug, pesticide, and pollutant evaluation; quality control; social science survey design and interpretation; political polling; and more.

The 18,000 U.S. statisticians in 1986 worked largely in private industry. Over half worked for manufacturing, insurance, and finance companies. The rest worked on campus, teaching and doing research, and for the federal government, especially for the Departments of Commerce, Labor, Health and Human Services, Agriculture, and Defense.

Many jobs are open to bachelor's graduates. Their starting pay runs between $15,000 and $18,000 per year. In 1987, the federal government started master's statisticians at $22,500 or $27,200 and new doctorates at $27,200 or $32,600. Federal statisticians averaged $39,400 in 1986. A 1985 survey found that doctoral statisticians averaged $43,700. Those on campus did slightly less well, at $42,200; those with the federal government did better, at $47,100.

For statisticians, the job outlook is favorable. Many jobs will be available in quality control, business forecasting, economics, management, the evaluation of drugs and other substances, and government programs. Much of the demand for statisticians is due to the ever-growing insistence on reducing risks of all kinds in safety-related fields, in health, and in business. This demand is not likely to change unless the costs of error fall drastically.

ACTUARIAL SCIENCE

Actuaries are statisticians who work for insurance companies and financial institutions. They calculate the probabilities of death, illness, disability, unemployment, retirement, and property loss. They use their calculations to compute expected payouts for insurance companies and pension funds and to set premiums that will allow their employers to make a profit. They may specialize in life, health, property, or liability insurance or in pension plans. As executives, they help set company policy. Actuaries who work for state and federal governments may work with government insurance and pension plans or serve as regulators of the private insurance and pension industries.

There were about 9,400 actuaries in 1986, most employed in the insurance industry. Only a few taught on campus. Almost all had a bachelor's degree in mathematics, statistics, or actuarial science; higher degrees were relatively scarce. Advancement depends on passing a series of examinations given by the Society of Actuaries, the Casualty Actuarial Society, and the American Society of Pension Actuaries. Preparation for the exams takes extensive home study, and the whole series of exams takes 5–10 years. Those who pass the whole series in their specialty become full members of their societies and earn the title of "fellow."

The job outlook for actuaries will be much better than the average for all occupations through the year 2000. The best opportunities will be for college graduates who have passed at least two of the actuarial exams while still in school. Many jobs will arise as the population ages and the demand for insurance increases, as the insurance industry changes, and as more states come to regulate the industry.

New bachelor's graduates who have passed none of the actuarial exams can expect to start at $19,000–24,000 per year. Passing one exam raises the starting pay to $21,000–25,000; passing two boosts it to $23,000–26,000. Actuaries who had progressed about halfway through the exam series in 1986 received $32,000 to $45,000. Actuarial fellows got $44,000–55,000. Further experience is worth even more; upper-level actuarial executives can top $60,000.

ACCOUNTING

The nation's 945,000 accountants and auditors are concerned with financial records. They keep track of expenditures, income, profit, and loss; prepare financial reports; and calculate taxes. Auditors tend to emphasize checking the financial records and reports of companies and individuals for conformity to truth and law.

Public accountants work for themselves or for accounting firms and prepare and audit financial records. *Management* (or industrial or private) *accountants* work for a company and handle its financial records. *Government accountants* and *auditors* deal with the records of government agencies and audit private companies and individuals; many work for the Internal Revenue Service.

Accountants may specialize in auditing, taxes, management consulting, or computer systems. Some serve business and professional schools as teachers, researchers, and administrators. A great many find the field congenial because there are many opportunities for part-time work, especially in small firms and in the preparation of tax returns.

Accountants can find jobs with degrees from business or correspondence schools, but most jobs require a bachelor's degree in accounting. Many employers ask for a master's. Most accountants find highly valuable the certificates in public accounting (CPA), management accounting, and internal auditing awarded upon examination by state boards of accountancy and the professional societies.

The job outlook is excellent, especially for accountants with computer experience. The pay started in 1986 at about $21,000 for beginning accountants and auditors. Experienced auditors can earn $30,000 to $40,000. Experienced, senior accountants can get $50,000 and up. In 1987, the federal government started junior accountants and auditors at $14,800. A superior academic record raised that to $18,400. A master's degree or two years of experience brought $22,500. In 1986, federal accountants and auditors averaged $35,000.

BOOKKEEPING

Bookkeepers and accounting clerks keep the financial records of businesses, prepare financial statements and bills, write checks, and calculate payrolls. In small businesses, they may have full responsibility for financial matters. In larger firms, they may work under a head bookkeeper or accountant.

Most of the nation's 2,100,000 bookkeeping jobs require no more than a high school diploma with courses in bookkeeping, business math, and accounting principles. The best opportunities go to graduates of bookkeeping programs at community colleges and business schools; experience with bookkeeping machines and computers helps greatly.

The U.S. Department of Labor expects bookkeeping employment to remain stable through the year 2000. However, employee turnover is high, so no bookkeeper need stay unemployed for long. In 1986, the pay began at $14,300 in private firms and went up to $17,000–18,000 with experience. In 1987, the federal government started bookkeepers with two years of experience or higher education at $13,248.

COMPUTER OPERATIONS

The computer industry employs a great many people, and it will need many more in the next few years as computers penetrate ever deeper into the fabric of modern civilization. At the highest levels, the field employs *information* and *computer scientists* in the design of new computers, computer languages, and related devices and in research into new ways to use computers effectively. These people often belong to the Institute of Electrical and Electronic Engineers (see Chapter 9). Some of their most exciting work is in the design of new and smaller integrated circuits or chips and in the field of artificial intelligence, where they strive to design machines that can imitate or duplicate various aspects of human intelligence, from pattern recognition to problem solving (in chess, geometry, algebra, and other areas).

At somewhat lower levels are the people who operate, program, and service computers. *Computer operators* enter data and instructions at typewriter keyboards and operate and control the computer, attaching peripheral equipment as necessary and watching for error signals. As *tape librarians,* they maintain files of data and programs on computer-readable magnetic media.

In 1986, there were about 263,000 computer operators. Employment in this field should rise much faster than the average for all occupations through the year 2000. The best opportunities will go to those who gain some post–high school training in computer operations in a community college, business school, or computer or vocational school. Training is also available in the military and on the job.

Most jobs that require relatively little education do not pay exceedingly well. There are exceptions, but computer operations is not one of them. In 1987, the federal government paid inexperienced computer operators only $12,500 a year. Experienced workers with supervisory duties can go higher; the federal average in 1986 was about $18,000. Better pay comes with further education and a change in job, perhaps to computer programmer.

COMPUTER PROGRAMMING

The 1986 roster of computer programmers included some 479,000 persons. Programmers are responsible for telling computers what to do with the data they are fed by their operators. Programmers write step-by-step instructions in one of many "computer languages." They must be able to think excruciatingly logically and to break down any process into its smallest steps.

Programmers work with mailing lists, payrolls, data bases, mathematical computations, and models of complex mechanical, economic, and weather systems. They invent video games, and they write the "software" packages that allow personal computers to balance budgets, compute statistics and taxes, and act as word processors. In every case, they must remove all errors from, or "debug," their programs so they will work. Their work ends with the preparation of instructions or documentation for the computer operator or the end user of the software.

Many computer programmers have bachelor's degrees in a field such as accounting, engineering, or mathematics, with additional courses in computer programming (offered today in almost every two-year and four-year school). Many more have bachelor's degrees in information or computer science; graduates with these degrees have increased in number from less than 20,000 per year in the early 1980s to over 40,000 per year in the late 1980s. Some jobs, especially on campus and in industrial or government research and development, require master's degrees or doctorates. Almost no jobs exist for programmers without some college education. Continuing education is essential for any programmer who wishes to keep up with the rapid changes in computer technology; courses are offered by employers, software (program) suppliers, and academic institutions.

There are many opportunities for advancement for skilled workers. In large organizations, programmers can move up to supervisory and management positions. Any programmer can cut loose to become a self-employed consultant or software specialist, often as part of the industry that has arisen to supply packaged programs for personal computers. The job prospects are excellent, with the field expected to grow much faster than average through the year 2000 and beyond. The best opportunities will be for men and women with bachelor's or higher degrees. People with two-year degrees will find their best prospects in business-related jobs.

In 1986, full-time programmers averaged about $27,000 per year. Highly skilled programmers earned over $43,000. In 1987, the federal government started new bachelor's graduate programmers at only $14,800.

COMPUTER SERVICE

Since computers are complex machines, they break down, and the computer industry depends heavily on computer service technicians—69,000 of them in 1986. These technicians diagnose and repair breakdowns in computers and their peripheral equipment (such as printers). They also perform routine maintenance—adjusting, cleaning, and oiling mechanical and electromechanical parts—and help install new equipment.

Computer service technicians are also called field or customer engineers, and the demand for them is very high. Some work for large computer users, who can expect enough malfunctions to keep one or more technicians busy. Many work for computer makers or lessors, working out of central offices to serve many computer users. Their pay averaged $26,700 in 1986. Senior technicians with several years of experience can expect over $40,000 per year.

The basic education for a job as a computer service technician requires one or two years of post–high school education in electronics or electrical engineering, obtained from a vocational school, a community college, or a four-year college or university. The necessary training is also available in the military. Further training on the job lasts six months to two years.

SYSTEMS ANALYSIS

The nation's 331,000 systems analysts work with business managers and scientific or technical specialists to define the nature of a data processing or calculation problem. They then break the problem into component parts; define necessary data, equipment, and processing steps; and instruct computer programmers in how to go about putting the problem "on the computer." They deal with a great variety of problems, from devising inventory systems and installing computers to forecasting sales and monitoring nuclear power plants. Some do research to devise new and more powerful methods of systems analysis.

Systems analysts generally need at least a bachelor's degree in whatever field they will work with most closely, plus plenty of course work in information or computer science or data processing. Some employers want the degree in a computer field, with lesser emphasis on the field of application. Many systems analysts have transferred from such other jobs as programmer. Graduate degrees are essential for the more complex jobs and for academic positions. Experience can lead to supervisory and management posts.

Employment in this field is expected to grow much faster than the average for all occupations through the year 2000. The federal government started new college graduates at about $15,000 in 1987. In 1986, systems analysts averaged almost $33,000 per year.

OPERATIONS RESEARCH

The nation's 38,000 operations research analysts deal with scheduling, forecasting, resource allocation, product mix, and distribution, using the principles of mathematics and logic to define organizational problems, break the problems into manageable pieces, and seek efficient, effective solutions. Their tools are the mathematics of linear programming and game theory, computer simulations, and systems analysis. They work intimately with both computers and the people whose work centers on the problems at issue. Since this kind of quantitative analysis is becoming more and more important in corporate and government decision making, employment in this field should expand much faster than the average for all occupations through the year 2000.

An operations research analyst must have a bachelor's degree in the field or in mathematics, statistics, economics, computer science, or some other highly quantitative field. But their training continues on the job, for new workers are often paired with experienced hands. Federal operations research analysts began at $14,800 in 1987, although a great academic record could boost that to $18,400. In 1986, federal operations analysts averaged $37,400 per year. All workers in this area, federal and nonfederal, averaged only $32,000.

THE HOT SPOTS

The best job outlook among mathematicians is for accountants, but even this group faces nowhere near the prospects of computer workers. Programmers, service technicians, and systems and operations research analysts all enjoy high pay and ample job opportunities, and the situation seems bound to get even better before it gets worse.

The reason is simple: computers represent an emerging technology. In the past 30 years, they have shrunk greatly in size and cost and grown tremendously in usefulness. Less than $100 will now buy more computing power than the founders of the field dreamed of, and it can fit in one hand rather than an entire air-conditioned building. Larger computers, many costing much less than a new car, are replacing and supplementing office desks at work and at home. And the technology is continuing to evolve.

At the same time, the falling costs and rising powers of computers mean that each generation of the machines finds more uses. It will not be many years before every business, large and small, and every educated individual has a computer. This penetration of the potential market is already well under way, and one side effect is a huge demand for writing about computers. There are already many computer magazines and a host of books for both experts and novices.

CAREERS ON CAMPUS

We have already noted that most pure mathematicians work as teachers and researchers at colleges and universities. Applied mathematicians usually find more lucrative employment in industry. The same goes for statisticians, actuaries, accountants, and computer people. There are, however, university and college positions in all of these fields. Teachers are essential, and each field advances at least in part by academic research. This is especially true for the computer sciences, for schools and departments of computer and information science are responsible for many of the latest improvements in computer science, including the fascinating progress that has been made in the field of artificial intelligence. Computer people, applied and pure mathematicians, and statisticians also find work in campus-affiliated and independent research centers. Too, many moonlight as consultants.

CAREERS IN INDUSTRY

Perhaps the best way to indicate the variety available in industrial careers in mathematics is to summarize a few of the industrial profiles described in *Profiles in Applied Mathematics*, a small booklet issued a few years ago by the Society for Industrial and Applied Mathematics. Other fields described in this chapter are so heavily industrial that their descriptions above adequately cover the careers available in them.

The Eastman Kodak Company, Analytical Methods Section of the Management Services Division, employed three doctorates (one in applied mathematics, one in operations research, and one in statistics), 37 MSs (25 in statistics; two each in applied mathematics, operations research, industrial engineering, computer science, and business; and one each in mathematics and chemical engineering), 11 BSs, 10 associate degrees, and nine nondegreed personnel. They worked in product development, experiment design and analysis, modeling, quality control, and market surveying.

The Chevron Research Company, Mathematics and Statistics Group, Computer and Systems Division, used one PhD mathematician, one PhD statistician, one MA mathematician, and one MS statistician for modeling, calculation, and software development.

The Bell Telephone Laboratories Research Development used seven PhD mathematicians to model crystal growth and wave behavior and develop computer systems.

The 59 staff members of the IBM Thomas J. Watson Research Center, Mathematical Sciences Department, included 23 mathematics PhDs, nine applied mathematics PhDs, and one each in communication science, logic, and operations research; one MS each in computer science and operations research; and 1.5 BSs in mathematics. They worked on both theoretical and practical aspects of computing.

Industrial careers pay quite well and can be very satisfying. In many areas, they offer the best or only way to deal with topics at the frontiers of knowledge and to do so with adequate equipment. IBM and Bell researchers, for instance, have far better facilities than do most researchers on campus.

CAREERS IN GOVERNMENT

Government needs actuaries, accountants, auditors, bookkeepers, computer operators, programmers, service technicians, systems and operations research analysts, mathematicians, and statisticians in every branch. Financial workers find jobs in the Internal Revenue Service, Treasury Department, and Office of Management and Budget, as well as on congressional staffs and in those parts of the Defense, Energy, Education, Interior, and other departments that deal with budgets. Mathematicians work for the Departments of Defense and Energy, and to a lesser extent elsewhere. Statisticans play vital roles in the Department of Commerce's National Bureau of Standards, Bureau of the Census, and Bureau of Economic Analysis; the Defense Department; the Department of Education's National Center for Education Statistics; the Department of Energy's Information Administration; the Department of Health and Human Services' National Center for Health Statistics and the National Institutes of Health; the Department of Justice's Bureau of Justice Statistics; the Department of Labor's Bureau of Labor Statistics; and many other agencies. At lower levels, they process the data on which the government runs. At higher levels, they may actually help make government policy.

ORGANIZATIONS FOR MATHEMATICIANS AND COMPUTER SCIENTISTS

Table 19 lists a number of organizations for mathematicians and computer scientists. Most offer career pamphlets for students and others contemplating the directions of their future lives. Many offer help in finding jobs. They may also offer lists of schools whose programs in their fields are approved or accredited. All hold periodic meetings at which members can exchange information, present papers, socialize, and seek jobs.

The American Mathematical Society offers the pamphlet *Seeking Employment in the Mathematical Sciences* for $2. The Mathematical Association of America offers *Professional Opportunities in Mathematics* for $2.

Table 19 Societies and sources of further information for mathematicians and computer scientists

American Mathematical Society
P.O. Box 6248
Providence, RI 02940

Mathematical Association of America
1529 18 Street NW
Washington, DC 20036

Society for Industrial and Applied Mathematics
1400 Architects Building
117 South 17 Street
Philadelphia, PA 19103

American Statistical Association
1429 Duke St.
Alexandria, VA 22314

American Society of Pension Actuaries
2029 K Street NW, 4th Floor
Washington, DC 20006

Casualty Actuarial Society
One Penn Plaza
250 West 34 Street
New York, NY 10119

Society of Actuaries
500 Park Blvd., Suite 440
Itasca, IL 60143

American Academy of Actuaries
1720 I St., NW, 7th Floor
Washington, DC 20006

National Association of Accountants
10 Paragon Dr.
Montvale, NJ 07645

National Society of Public Accountants and Accreditation Council for Accountancy
1010 North Fairfax Street
Alexandria, VA 22314

Institute of Internal Auditors
P.O. Box 1119
249 Maitland Avenue
Altamonte Springs, FL 32701

American Federation of Information Processing Societies
1899 Preston White Dr.
Reston, VA 22091

Association for Systems Management
24587 Bagley Road
Cleveland, OH 44138

Institute of Electrical and Electronics Engineers, Inc.
345 East 47 Street
New York, NY 10017

Institute of Mathematical Statistics
3401 Investment Blvd., No. 7
Hayward, CA 94545

Table 19 (continued)

The Operations Research Society of America
Mount Royal and Guilford Ave.
Baltimore, MD 21202

American Institute of Certified Public Accountants
1211 Avenue of the Americas
New York, NY 10036-8775

The EDP Auditors Association
P.O. Box 88180
Carol Stream, IL 60188-0180

FINDING JOBS

11

As the last few chapters have made abundantly clear, there are a great many different possible careers in science. They require various levels of education, and they offer various degrees of pay. Some offer great room for advancement; some do not. Most offer recognition and the sense of self-worth that comes from knowing that one is doing useful, challenging work.

Many scientists find that the greatest advantage of their work is the feeling that they are not performing "just another job." Unlike workers in many other areas, they do not have to wait for weekends, vacations, and retirement to do what they really enjoy. They are already doing what they enjoy most, and they are getting paid for it.

Many people find that a career in science is more than a career. It is a way of life that provides the scientist's most valued pleasures, achievements, and gratifications. It is thus, perhaps, what any career *should* be, but too few are—demanding, absorbing, and fulfilling. Teachers are committed to educating young people, both in and out of the classroom. Researchers and technicians are constantly thinking of problems and solutions; their work, like other people's hobbies, even enters their dinner-table and party conversations. The scientist's work is never far from his or her mind; a scientist never willingly drops it. Scientists need never find their work boring, unless they are in the wrong field, and they don't retire easily.

It is possible for a scientist to do research and teach informally, without an actual scientific job. Once upon a time, in fact, this was how scientists survived. They were theologians, monks, philosophers, cloth merchants, and bureaucrats who pursued their science on the side, as a hobby. They were "amateurs," lovers of their fields, unpaid except in satisfaction and—sometimes—fame. They accomplished wonders, and they laid the foundations of modern science.

But a job is a great help. It allows more time for the field one loves. It often carries with it better equipment and facilities, easier access to colleagues, and a greater variety of rewards. And fortunately, science today is a professional activity, not a hobby. The scientist is expected to work as a scientist.

So how do scientists find suitable jobs? How do they locate their professional niche? They choose their field. They obtain all the training needed. Now, how do they find that first job—an entry position?

At the lowest levels, this question has a simple answer. High school graduates find jobs as bookkeepers, for instance, by answering ads in newspapers. So can technicians, teachers, and researchers, but for them there are more fruitful avenues as well. The best of these avenues may be the one that starts with "contacts"—everyone can use it, from high school grads to PhDs.

CONTACTS

Earlier in this book we stressed that college and graduate students can both gain valuable experience and pay some of their educational bills by working part-time and summers as research or teaching assistants. They may work for a faculty member at their school or at a nearby lab, museum, or other institution. They may find work by asking one of their professors or by replying to an on-campus announcement. College and university departments and school financial aid or placement offices may post lists of available part-time and summer positions.

Finding work in such ways depends on being in the right place, close to the right people, at the right time. This is the essence of the "contact"—someone who knows the job seeker and whom the job seeker can reach easily. And contacts can be a great help later on too. As students near graduation, many of them find that their departments, their faculty advisers, or the professors they work for know of fellowships, postdoctoral positions, and teaching and research jobs in the academic world, in government, and in industry. That knowledge may come from fliers mailed out by employers looking for new graduates or from colleagues elsewhere who have asked, "Do you know someone good for this job?" A recommendation from a professor whom an employer knows and trusts may be the best possible credential for a job.

Students can find it a great help to attend scientific meetings in their fields whenever possible. On these occasions, they will meet many people and establish their own contacts. They will find that many of the people they meet have their ears open for job opportunities, while others are looking for potential employees. The main purpose of scientific meetings is supposedly the exchange of scientific information, but it is sometimes said that job hunting gets just as much, or more, attention.

Are contacts useful only at the beginning of a working career? Not at all. They may very well help match the student with a first job, but then the student begins to establish a reputation as a teacher, researcher, technician, administrator, or whatever. The worker becomes known to others in the field, and finds that prospective employers approach him or her at meetings or by phone or mail. These employers are drawn by the reputation, or they were given the worker's name by a past professor or a mutual friend. Perhaps they were co-workers in the past, or they were once met and then forgotten. In all such cases, the potential job comes because of contacts that the worker has made in the past.

"Contacts" jobs may be the best ones. They usually seem to mean that someone who knows both the job and the worker has thought that the two belong together, and that someone is often right. "Noncontacts" jobs carry at best only a vague possibility that the worker and the job will get along.

It is thus a good idea to cultivate all the contacts possible. Students should work with their professors. Students and graduates should attend meetings, meet people, and join research, engineering, design, and other kinds of teams. They should never work alone if they can avoid it, for that insulates them from contacts and may limit their future choice of jobs.

CAMPUS PLACEMENT OFFICES

Many two-year, four-year, and graduate schools have placement offices. They may list mainly jobs on campus open to students. They may also list off-campus jobs open to present students and recent graduates. In the latter case, the placement office is more useful to the new worker seeking a career position in industry or on another campus.

Placement offices also help students prepare their résumés. This is a straight-forward enough task, and there are a great many available sources of information on how to do it, from "professional writing" textbooks to job-hunting manuals. However, it is also a task that baffles many young job seekers, and the help in preparing résumés that campus placement offices offer prompts many students to bless them.

Finally, placement offices—especially those at larger schools—often arrange for prospective employers in industry and government to send "recruiters" to campus. They set a date for, say, "Campus Career Days." The recruiters arrive together, and they may all have booths or tables in one location, such as the school gym. They then interview interested students who are near graduation. When they find students whose backgrounds, educations, talents, and interests match vacant niches in their organizations, they may invite these students to visit their headquarters for further interviews. They may, on occasion, make actual job offers on the spot, and fortunate students (mostly in engineering and the computer sciences) may have their pick of 30 or more job offers.

INQUIRIES

Getting a job, whether through contacts, through placement offices, or by answering ads, requires some initial approach. It may be face-to-face at a professional meeting, by phone, or—most often—by mail. Job seekers generally write letters of inquiry. These letters describe the job seeker and his or her background, say what job the seeker wants as specifically as possible, and say what good the job seeker can do the employer.

If a colleague, professor, or friend has suggested contacting the employer, the letter should say so. It should be addressed to some specific person at the employer's office, and it should make clear that the job seeker knows something about the employer's operations and has some idea of how he or she might fit in.

For example, Janine Latrobe is a geophysical consultant working out of Detroit. Peter Jeffers, a friend who works as a geologist for GeoSystems, Inc., in Tucson, writes to say that his firm has just accepted a contract to build a geothermal energy plant. He remembers that Janine has been involved with similar projects in the past. Would she be interested in coming to Tucson? They will be needing a head for the design team. The chief of the engineering department is Iosip Wilkov.

Janine is interested, and she writes directly to Iosip Wilkov, not to the personnel department. She says something along these lines:

> Peter Jeffers, a GeoSystems geologist, recently wrote me that you will soon begin work on a geothermal energy plant and may need a geophysicist to lead your design team.
>
> As a geophysical consultant for the last nine years, I have worked with some very challenging geothermal projects. In one, the problem was high-pressure fluids. In another, it was very corrosive fluids. In both cases, I helped find the solution. You can call [names, phone numbers, company names] if you have any questions about my competence.
>
> Mr. Jeffers did not tell me a great deal about your particular geothermal energy project, but I am confident that I can help. I would be delighted to talk with you to learn the details and to fill out a formal application for the job.

She then says when she can come to Tucson, describes current projects she is working on, and encloses her résumé and letters of recommendation. She is confident—as she should be—that her letter will be far more effective than one that fails to relate her to both the employer and the job. The only thing she might have done differently would have been to call Iosip Wilkov first to learn some of the details of the job and confirm that there was indeed an opening. In her letter, she could then have related herself to the details. She could also have begun her letter with a more personal touch, "As we discussed on the phone yesterday..."

Answering job ads is a little more difficult. The ads often spend a paragraph describing the job, but they don't reveal a great deal of detail. Again, a phone call can help. If one has a friend who works for the advertising employer, calling that friend can reveal details such as specific projects or goals that the "contact name" in the ad might not even know. Such details can help a job seeker write a very convincing letter.

PROFESSIONAL SOCIETIES

Like colleges and universities, professional societies often run placement services. Many publish journals that list job openings. The American Association for the Advancement of Science (AAAS) publishes *Science,* whose ads cover the gamut of disciplines and employers—academic, industrial, and government. The *Chronicle of Higher Education* and the *Bulletin of the American Association of University Professors* concentrate on academic posts.

The American Institute of Biological Sciences (AIBS) runs ads for the biological sciences in its journal, *Bioscience.* Both the AIBS and the Federation of American Societies for Experimental Biology (FASEB) run placement services that are available to both members and nonmembers. Both job seekers and employee seekers register with these services, and lists of each are made available each year. These services also arrange candidate-employer interviews at the annual meetings of the AIBS and the FASEB, and every year hundreds of young biologists meet their employers in this way. For further information, write to:

FASEB Placement Service   AIBS
9650 Rockville Pike   730 11th Street, NW
Bethesda, MD 20814   Washington, DC 20001-4584

In the earth sciences, job ads appear in *EOS,* the weekly newsmagazine of the American Geophysical Union, and in the monthly newsletter of the American Meteorological Society. The Geological Society of America runs a computer matching service for job seekers (GSA Employment Matching Service, PO Box 9140, 3300 Penrose Place, Boulder, CO 80301).

The American Chemical Society runs job ads for chemists in its weekly *Chemical and Engineering News.* It also runs an Employment Clearing House and an Employment Aids Office (ACS, 1155 16 Street NW, Washington, DC 20036).

For the space sciences, the American Astronomical Society runs a job service consisting of a monthly Job Register, a Candidates Register of Résumés, and a Job Center at the society's meetings. The American Institute of Aeronautics and Astronautics offers *The AIAA Employment Workshop Handbook* and *Job Hunting: The Seven Steps to Success,* and it runs employment workshops in regions of the country hit by high unemployment among its members. Employers attend the meetings of the American Astronautical Society to look for employees. The physics, engineering, and mathematics societies offer similar kinds of help.

Anyone looking for a job through ads should not neglect the larger newspapers and the weekend editions of smaller ones. They too advertise a wealth of positions on campus, in industry, and in government, in all fields and at all levels. The difference is that many of their ads are for jobs in the newspaper's city, state, or region, which can prove very useful to the job seeker who wants to settle or remain in a particular locale.

THE FEDERAL SYSTEM

The federal government fills some of its positions through contacts and journal and newspaper ads. Most often, however, it relies on the U.S. Office of Personnel Management (OPM). The OPM process is both simple and attractive, for it allows a job seeker to apply for many jobs at once. Most states have similar systems.

The Postal Service, FBI, and CIA have their own procedures, and jobs that exist in only one government agency require application directly to the agency. The U.S. Department of Agriculture has so many unique jobs that it runs a fairly elaborate system of its own. For jobs in the Soil Conservation Service, one should write the Special Examining Unit, 1000 Aerospace Road, Lanham, MD 20801. For jobs in the Science and Education Administration, one should write the Special Examining Unit, 6505 Belcrest Road, Hyattsville, MD 20782.

The first step in the OPM process is to call or write a Federal Job Information Center and describe one's education and experience, the kind of work wanted, the locale preferred, the lowest salary acceptable, and the dates of one's military service (veterans enjoy preference). The center then says whether any applications are being accepted for any jobs that might fit. If so, the job seeker fills out a series of forms, a thesis description, and a list of publications and reports. He or she then mails the completed forms to a U.S. Office of Personnel Management area office (see Table 20).

On receipt of the forms, the OPM evaluates the applicant. If the jobs sought are filled on the basis of competitive performance on written tests, it asks the applicant to take the tests. The score on these tests determines one's place on an OPM "referral list." If the jobs sought do not require tests, the OPM rates the applicant according to the qualifications described on the forms and adds the applicant's name to the civil service list. The applicant remains on this list for one year unless he or she updates the application every 10–12 months.

Later, when some government agency comes up with appropriate vacancies, the OPM gives that agency a list of the qualified applicants. The agency makes its choices, invites applicants for interviews, and makes job offers. GS grade and pay depend more on the job than on one's qualifications (see Chapter 5). Advancement follows with experience and further education or training, just as it does on campus and in industry.

Table 20 U.S. Office of Personnel Management regional offices

10 Causeway St.
Boston, MA 02222-1031

26 Federal Plaza
New York, NY 10278

600 Arch St.
Philadelphia, PA 19106

75 Spring St. SW
Atlanta, GA 30303-3109

230 S. Dearborn St.
Chicago, IL 60604

1100 Commerce St.
Dallas, TX 75242

815 Olive St.
St. Louis, MO 63101

7th Fl., 211 Main St.
San Francisco, CA 94105

BIBLIOGRAPHY

Ayre, P., and P. M. Lemaire. *Careers Nontraditional.* Washington, DC: American Chemical Society, 1977.

Babco, E. L. *Salaries of Scientists, Engineers, and Technicians: A Summary of Salary Surveys,* 13th ed. Washington, DC: Scientific Manpower Commission, October 1987.

Campbell, P. N., ed. *Biology in Profile: A Guide to the Many Branches of Biology.* Elmsford, NY: Pergamon Press, 1981.

Cole, J. R. "Women in Science." *American Scientist* 69 (July–August 1981), pp. 385–91.

A Counselor's Guide to Occupational Information. U.S. Department of Labor, Bureau of Labor Statistics, Bulletin 2042, July 1980.

Culliton, B. J. "The Academic-Industrial Complex." *Science,* May 28, 1982, pp. 960–62.

Easton, T. A. *Working for Life: Careers in Biology.* Medford, NJ: Plexus, 1983; 2d ed., 1988.

Hawking, S. W. *A Brief History of Time: From the Big Bang to Black Holes.* New York: Bantam Books, 1988.

Healy, C. C. *Career Development: Counseling through the Life Stages.* Boston: Allyn & Bacon, 1982.

Holland, J. L. *Making Vocational Choices: A Theory of Careers.* Englewood Cliffs, NJ: Prentice-Hall, 1973.

———. *The Self-Directed Search.* Palo Alto, CA: Consulting Psychologists Press, 1977.

———. *Understanding Yourself and Your Career.* Palo Alto, CA: Consulting Psychologists Press, 1977.

———. *Vocational Choice.* Waltham, MA: Waltham Press, 1966.

Kutscher, R. E. "An overview of the year 2000," *Occupational Outlook Quarterly,* Spring 1988, pp. 3–9.

Medawar, P. B. *Advice to a Young Scientist.* New York: Harper & Row, 1979.

Moravec, H. *Mind Children: The Future of Robot and Human Intelligence.* Cambridge, MA: Harvard University Press, 1988.

Occupational Outlook Handbook. U.S. Department of Labor, Bureau of Labor Statistics, Bulletin 2300, April 1988.

Postdoctoral Appointments and Disappointments. Washington, DC: National Research Council, 1981.

Science and Engineering Employment: 1970–80. Special Report NSF 81–310. Washington, DC: National Science Foundation, 1981.

Sheffield, C., and C. Rosin. *Space Careers.* New York: William Morrow, 1983.

Super, D. E. *The Psychology of Careers.* New York: Harper & Row, 1957.

Vetter, B. M. *A Statistical Report on Black Americans in Science.* Washington, DC: AAAS Office of Opportunities in Science, 1981.

Vetter, B. M. *The Technological Marketplace: Supply and Demand for Scientists and Engineers,* 3rd ed. Washington, DC: Scientific Manpower Commission, May 1985.

Vetter, B. M., and E. L. Babco, *Professional Women and Minorities: A Manpower Data Resource Service,* 7th ed. Washington, DC: Commission on Professionals in Science and Technology (was Scientific Manpower Commission), December 1987.

White, M. C. "The 1988–89 job outlook in brief." *Occupational Outlook Quarterly,* Spring 1988, pp. 10–45.

Women and Minorities in Science and Engineering. Washington, DC: National Science Foundation, January 1986 (NSF 86-301).

Special Issues of *Scientific American:* "The Dynamic Earth," September 1983; "Computer Software," September 1984; "The Molecules of Life," October 1985; "Materials for Economic Growth," October 1986; "The Next Computer Revolution," October 1987.

APPENDIX

STATE EDUCATIONAL AGENCIES (SOURCES OF INFORMATION ON GUARANTEED STUDENT LOANS, PLUS LOANS, SLS LOANS, AND STATE STUDENT AID)

Alabama

Alabama Commission on Higher Education
1 Court Square, Suite 221
Montgomery, Alabama
36197-0001
GSL/PLUS/SLS and **State Aid:**
(205) 269-2700

Alaska

Alaska Commission on Postsecondary Education
400 Willoughby Avenue
Box FP
Juneau, Alaska 99811
GSL/PLUS/SLS and **State Aid:**
(907) 465-2854

Arizona

GSL/PLUS/SLS:
Arizona Educational Loan Program
2600 North Central Avenue, Suite 621
Phoenix, Arizona 85004
(800) 352-3033 (AZ students only)
(602) 252-5793

Source: *The Student Guide: Five Federal Financial Aid Programs* (Washington, DC: U.S. Department of Education, 1988).

State Aid:
Commission for Postsecondary Education
3030 North Central Avenue, Suite 1407
Phoenix, Arizona 85012
(602) 255-3109

Arkansas

GSL/PLUS/SLS:
Student Loan Guarantee Foundation of Arkansas
219 South Victory
Little Rock, Arkansas
72201-1884
(501) 372-1491

State Aid: Department of Higher Education
1220 West 3rd Street
Little Rock, Arkansas 72201
(501) 371-1441

California

California Student Aid Commission
P.O. Box 945625
Sacramento, California 94245-0625
GSL/PLUS/SLS:
(916) 323-0435

State Aid:
P.O. Box 942845
Sacramento, California 94245-0845
(916) 445-0880

Colorado

GSL/PLUS/SLS:
Colorado Guaranteed Student Loan Program
11990 Grant, Suite 500
North Glenn, Colorado 80233
(303) 450-9333

State Aid: Colorado Commission on Higher Education
Colorado Heritage Center
1300 Broadway, 2nd Floor
Denver, Colorado 80203
(303) 866-2723

Connecticut

GSL/PLUS/SLS:
Connecticut Student Loan Foundation
25 Pratt Street
Hartford, Connecticut 06103
(203) 547-1510

State Aid: Connecticut Department of Higher Education
61 Woodland Station
Hartford, Connecticut
06105-2391
(203) 566-2618

Delaware

Delaware Higher Education Loan Program
Carvel State Office Building
820 North French Street
4th Floor
Wilmington, Delaware 19801
GSL/PLUS/SLS:
(302) 571-6055
State Aid: (302) 571-3240

District of Columbia

GSL/PLUS/SLS:
Higher Education Loan Program of Washington, DC
1023 15th St., NW
10th Floor
Suite 1000
Washington, DC 20005
(202) 289-4500

State Aid: Office of Postsecondary Education Research and Assistance
D. C. Department of Human Services
1331 H Street, NW
Suite 600
Washington, DC 20005
(202) 727-3688

Florida

Office of Student Financial Assistance
Department of Education
Knott Building
Tallahassee, Florida 32399
GSL/PLUS/SLS:
(904) 488-8093
State Aid: (904) 488-6181

Georgia   Georgia Student Finance Commission
                     2082 East Exchange Place
                     Suite 200
                     Tucker, Georgia 30084
                     GSL/PLUS/SLS:
                     (404) 493-5468
                     State Aid: (404) 493-5444

Hawaii   **GSL/PLUS/SLS:**
                     Hawaii Education Loan Program
                     PO Box 22187
                     Honolulu, Hawaii 96822-0187
                     (808) 546-3731

                     State Aid: State Postsecondary Education Commission
                     209 Bachman Hall
                     University of Hawaii
                     2444 Dole Street
                     Honolulu, Hawaii 96822
                     (808) 948-8213

Idaho   **GSL/PLUS/SLS:** Student Loan Fund of Idaho, Inc.
                     Processing Center
                     PO Box 730
                     Fruitland, Idaho 83619
                     (208) 452-4058

                     State Aid: Office of State Board of Education
                     650 West State Street
                     Room 307
                     Boise, Idaho 83720
                     (208) 334-2270

Illinois   Illinois State Scholarship Commission
                     106 Wilmot Road
                     Deerfield, Illinois 60015
                     GSL/PLUS/SLS and **State Aid:**
                     (312) 948-8550

Indiana   State Student Assistance Commission of Indiana
                       964 North Pennsylvania Street
                       Indianapolis, Indiana 46204
                       GSL/PLUS/SLS:
                       (317) 232-2366
                       State Aid: (317) 232-2351

Iowa   Iowa College Aid Commission
                       201 Jewett Building
                       9th and Grand Avenue
                       Des Moines, Iowa 50309
                       GSL/PLUS/SLS:
                       (515) 281-4890
                       State Aid: (515) 281-3501

Kansas   **GSL/PLUS/SLS:**
                       Higher Education Assistance Foundation
                       6800 College Blvd.
                       Suite 600
                       Overland Park, Kansas 66211-1532
                       (913) 345-1300

                       State Aid: Kansas Board of Regents
                       Suite 609, Capitol Tower
                       400 SW 8th
                       Topeka, Kansas 66603
                       (913) 296-3517

Kentucky   Kentucky Higher Education Assistance Authority
                       1050 U.S. 127 South
                       Frankfort, Kentucky 40601
                       GSL/PLUS/SLS and **State Aid:**
                       (502) 564-7990

Louisiana   Governor's Special Commission on Education Services
                       PO Box 44127
                       Capitol Station
                       Baton Rouge, Louisiana 70804
                       GSL/PLUS/SLS and **State Aid:**
                       (504) 342-9415

Maine   Maine Department of Educational and Cultural Services
                                 Division of Higher Education Services
                                 State House Station 119
                                 Augusta, Maine 04333
                                 GSL/PLUS/SLS and **State Aid:**
                                 (207) 289-2183

Maryland   **GSL/PLUS/SLS:**
                                 Maryland Higher Education Loan Corporation
                                 2100 Guilford Avenue
                                 Room 305
                                 Baltimore, Maryland 21218
                                 (301) 333-6555

                                 State Aid: Maryland State Scholarship Board
                                 2100 Guilford Avenue
                                 2nd Floor, Room 207
                                 Baltimore, Maryland 21218
                                 (301) 333-6420

Massachusetts   **GSL/PLUS/SLS:**
                                 Massachusetts Higher Education Assistance Corporation
                                 Berkeley Place
                                 330 Stuart Street
                                 Boston, Massachusetts 02116
                                 (617) 426-9434

                                 State Aid:
                                 The Board of Regents of Higher Education Scholarship Office
                                 150 Causeway Street
                                 Room 600
                                 Boston, Massachusetts 02114
                                 (617) 727-9420

Michigan   **GSL/PLUS/SLS:**
                                 Michigan Department of Education Guaranteed Student Loan Program
                                 Box 30047
                                 Lansing, Michigan 48909
                                 (517) 373-0760

State Aid: Michigan Department of Education
P.O. Box 30008
Lansing, Michigan 48909
(517) 373-3394

Minnesota

GSL/PLUS/SLS:
Higher Education Assistance Foundation
85 East 7th Street
Suite 500
St. Paul, Minnesota 55101
(612) 227-7661

State Aid: Minnesota Higher Education Coordinating Board
Capitol Square, Suite 400
550 Cedar Street
St. Paul, Minnesota 55101
(612) 296-3974

Mississippi

GSL/PLUS/SLS:
Mississippi Guarantee Student Loan Agency
3825 Ridgewood Road
PO Box 342
Jackson, Mississippi 39205-0342
(601) 982-6663

State Aid: Mississippi Postsecondary Education Financial Assistance
   Board
PO Box 2336
Jackson, Mississippi 39225-2336
(601) 982-6570

Missouri

Coordinating Board for Higher Education
PO Box 1438
Jefferson City, Missouri 65102
GSL/PLUS/SLS and **State Aid:**
(314) 751-3940

Montana

Montana University System
33 South Last Chance Gulch
Helena, Montana 59620-3104
GSL/PLUS/SLS and **State Aid:**
(406) 444-6594

Nebraska

GSL/PLUS/SLS:
Higher Education Assistance Foundation
Cornhusker Bank Building
11th and Cornhusker Highway
Suite 304
Lincoln, Nebraska 68521
(402) 476-9129

State Aid: Nebraska Coordinating Commission for Postsecondary
   Education
PO Box 95005
Lincoln, Nebraska 68509-5005
(402) 471-2847

Nevada

GSL/PLUS/SLS:
NGSLP Nevada State Department of Education
400 West King Street
Capitol Complex
Carson City, Nevada 89710
(702) 885-5914

State Aid: Student Services
Student Financial Aid Services
University of Nevada-Reno
Room 200 TSSC
Reno, Nevada 89557-0072
(702) 784-4666

New Hampshire

GSL/PLUS/SLS:
New Hampshire Higher Education Assistance Foundation
PO Box 877
Concord, New Hampshire 03302
(603) 225-6612

State Aid: New Hampshire
   Postsecondary Education Commission
2¹/₂ Beacon Street
Concord, New Hampshire 03301
(603) 271-2555

New Jersey

GSL/PLUS/SLS:
New Jersey Higher Education Assistance Authority
C. N. 543
Trenton, New Jersey 08625
(609) 588-3200

State Aid: Department of Higher Education
Office of Student Assistance
4 Quarkerbridge Plaza
C. N. 540
Trenton, New Jersey 08625
1-(800) 792-8670

New Mexico

GSL/PLUS/SLS:
New Mexico Educational Assistance Foundation
PO Box 27020
Albuquerque, New Mexico 87125-7020
(505) 345-3371

State Aid: Commission on Higher Education
1068 Cerrillos Road
Sante Fe, New Mexico 87501-4295
(505) 827-8300

New York

New York State Higher Education Services Corporation
99 Washington Avenue
Albany, New York 12255
GSL/PLUS/SLS:
(518) 473-1574
State Aid: (518) 474-5642

North Carolina

North Carolina State Education Assistance Authority
PO Box 2688
Chapel Hill, North Carolina 27515-2688
GSL/PLUS/SLS and **State Aid:**
(919) 549-8614

North Dakota

GSL/PLUS/SLS:
Bank of North Dakota Student Loan Department
PO Box No. 5509
Bismarck, North Dakota 58502-5509
(701) 224-5600

State Aid: North Dakota Student Financial Assistance Program
10th Floor, State Capitol
Bismarck, North Dakota 58505-0154
(701) 224-4114

Ohio

GSL/PLUS/SLS:
Ohio Student Loan Commission
PO Box 16610
Columbus, Ohio 43266-0610
(614) 466-3091

State Aid: Ohio Board of Regents
Student Assistance Office
3600 State Office Tower
30 East Broad Street
Columbus, Ohio 43216
(614) 466-7420

Oklahoma

Oklahoma State Regents for Higher Education
500 Education Building
State Capitol Complex
Oklahoma City, Oklahoma 73105
GSL/PLUS/SLS:
(405) 521-8262
State Aid: (405) 525-8180

Oregon

Oregon State Scholarship Commission
1445 Willamette Street
Eugene, Oregon 97401
1-(800) 452-8807
(within Oregon)
GSL/PLUS/SLS:
(503) 686-3200
State Aid: (503) 686-4166

Pennsylvania

Pennsylvania Higher Education Assistance Agency
660 Boas Street
Harrisburg, Pennsylvania 17102
GSL/PLUS/SLS:
1-(800) 692-7392
State Aid:
1-(800) 692-7435

Rhode Island   Rhode Island Higher Education Assistance Authority
                              560 Jefferson Boulevard
                              Warwick, Rhode Island 02886
                              GSL/PLUS/SLS and **State Aid:**
                              (401) 277-2050
                              Out of State Toll Free
                              1-(800) 922-9855

South Carolina   **GSL/PLUS/SLS:**
                              South Carolina Student Loan Corporation
                              Interstate Center, Suite 210
                              PO Box 21487
                              Columbia, South Carolina 29221
                              (803) 798-0916

                              State Aid: Higher Education Tuition Grants Agency
                              411 Keenan Building
                              Box 12159
                              Columbia, South Carolina 29211
                              (803) 734-1200

South Dakota   **GSL/PLUS/SLS:**
                              Education Assistance Corporation
                              115 First Avenue, S.W.
                              Aberdeen, South Dakota 57401
                              (605) 225-6423

                              State Aid: Department of Education and Cultural Affairs
                              Richard F. Kneip Building
                              700 Governors Drive
                              Pierre, South Dakota 57501-2293
                              (605) 773-3134

Tennessee   Tennessee Student Assistance Corporation
                              400 James Robertson Parkway
                              Suite 1950, Parkway Tower
                              Nashville, Tennessee 37219-5097
                              GSL/PLUS/SLS and **State Aid:**
                              [within TN 1-(800) 342-1663]
                              (615) 741-1346

Texas

GSL/PLUS/SLS:
Texas Guaranteed Student Loan Corporation
PO Box 15996
Austin, Texas 78761
(512) 835-1900

State Aid: Texas Higher Education Coordinating Board, Texas College
and University System
PO Box 12788
Austin, Texas 78711
(512) 462-6400

Utah

GSL/PLUS/SLS:
Loan Servicing Corp. of Utah
PO Box 30802
Salt Lake City, Utah 84130-0802
(801) 363-9151

State Aid: Utah State Board of Regents
3 Triad Center
Suite 550
355 West North Temple
Salt Lake City, Utah 84180-1205
(801) 538-5247

Vermont

Vermont Student Assistance Corporation
Champlain Mill
PO Box 2000
Winooski, Vermont 05404-2000
GSL/PLUS/SLS and **State Aid:**
[within VT 1-(800) 642-3177]
(802) 655-9602

Virginia

GSL/PLUS/SLS:
State Education Assistance Authority
6 North Sixth Street
Suite 300
Richmond, Virginia 23219
(804) 786-2035

State Aid: State Council of Higher Education for Virginia
James Monroe Building
101 N. 14th Street
Richmond, Virginia 23219
(804) 225-2141

Washington

GSL/PLUS/SLS:
Washington Student Loan Guaranty Association
500 Colman Building
811 First Avenue
Seattle, Washington 98104
(206) 625-1030

State Aid: Higher Education Coordinating Board
908 East Fifth Avenue
Olympia, Washington 98504
Attn: Financial Aid Office
(206) 753-3571

West Virginia

GSL/PLUS/SLS:
Higher Education Assistance Foundation
Higher Education Loan Program of West Virginia, Inc.
PO Box 591
Charleston, West Virginia 25322
(304) 345-7211

State Aid: West Virginia Board of Regents
PO Box 4007
Charleston, West Virginia 25364
(304) 347-1211

Wisconsin

GSL/PLUS/SLS:
Wisconsin Higher Education Corporation
2401 International Lane
Madison, Wisconsin 53704
(608) 246-1800

State Aid: Wisconsin Higher Educational Aids Board
PO Box 7885
Madison, Wisconsin 53707
(608) 267-2206

Wyoming

GSL/PLUS/SLS:
Higher Education Assistance Foundation
American National Bank Building
1912 Capitol Ave.
Suite 320
Cheyenne, Wyoming 82001
(307) 635-3259

State Aid: Wyoming Community College Commission
2301 Central Avenue
Barrett Building, 3rd Floor
Cheyenne, Wyoming 82002
(307) 777-7763

American Samoa

GSL/PLUS/SLS:
Pacific Islands Educational Loan Program
United Student Aid Funds, Inc.
1314 South King Street
Suite 961
Honolulu, Hawaii 96814
(808) 536-3731

State Aid: American Samoa Community College
PO Box 2609
Pago Pago, American Samoa 96799
(684) 699-9155

Northern Mariana Islands

GSL/PLUS/SLS: See American Samoa

State Aid: Northern Marianas College
Board of Regents
PO Box 1250
Saipan, CM 96950
(Saipan) 670-7542

Federated States of Micronesia, Marshall Islands, Republic of Palau

GSL/PLUS/SLS: See American Samoa

State Aid: Community College of Micronesia
PO Box 159
Kolonia, Ponape, F.S.M. 96941
(Ponape) 480 or 479

Micronesian Occupational College
PO Box 9
Koror, Palau 96940
471

Virgin Islands   Virgin Islands Board of Education
                              PO Box 11900
                              St. Thomas, Virgin Islands 00801
                              GSL/PLUS/SLS and **State Aid:**
                              (809) 774-4546

USAF, Inc.   United Student Aid Funds Processing Center
                              PO Box 50827
                              Indianapolis, Indiana 46250
                              (800) 382-4506 (within IN)
                              (800) 824-7044

Guam   **GSL/PLUS/SLS:** See American Samoa

                              State Aid: University of Guam
                              UOG Station
                              Mangilao, Guam 96913
                              (671) 734-2921

Puerto Rico   **GSL/PLUS/SLS:**
                              Higher Education Assistance Corporation
                              PO Box 42001
                              Minillas Station
                              San Juan, Puerto Rico 00940-2001
                              (809) 758-3356/3328

                              State Aid: Council on Higher Education
                              Box F-UPR Station
                              San Juan, Puerto Rico 00931
                              (809) 758-3356/3328

INDEX

VGM CAREER BOOKS

OPPORTUNITIES IN

*Available in both
paperback and hardbound
editions*
Accounting Careers
Acting Careers
Advertising Careers
Agriculture Careers
Airline Careers
Animal and Pet Care
Appraising Valuation Science
Architecture
Automotive Service
Banking
Beauty Culture
Biological Sciences
Biotechnology Careers
Book Publishing Careers
Broadcasting Careers
Building Construction Trades
Business Communication Careers
Business Management
Cable Television
Carpentry Careers
Chemical Engineering
Chemistry Careers
Child Care Careers
Chiropractic Health Care
Civil Engineering Careers
Commercial Art and Graphic
 Design
Computer Aided Design
 and Computer Aided Mfg.
Computer Maintenance Careers
Computer Science Careers
Counseling & Development
Crafts Careers
Dance
Data Processing Careers
Dental Care
Drafting Careers
Electrical Trades
Electronic and Electrical
 Engineering
Energy Careers
Engineering Technology Careers
Environmental Careers
Fashion Careers
Fast Food Careers
Federal Government Careers
Film Careers
Financial Careers
Fire Protection Services
Fitness Careers
Food Services
Foreign Language Careers
Forestry Careers
Gerontology Careers
Government Service
Graphic Communications
Health and
 Medical Careers
High Tech Careers
Home Economics Careers
Hospital Administration
Hotel & Motel Management
Human Resources Management
 Careers

Industrial Design
Insurance Careers
Interior Design
International Business
Journalism Careers
Landscape Architecture
Laser Technology
Law Careers
Law Enforcement and
 Criminal Justice
Library and Information
 Science
Machine Trades
Magazine Publishing Careers
Management
Marine & Maritime Careers
Marketing Careers
Materials Science
Mechanical Engineering
Medical Technology Careers
Microelectronics
Military Careers
Modeling Careers
Music Careers
Newspaper Publishing
 Careers
Nursing Careers
Nutrition Careers
Occupational Therapy
 Careers
Office Occupations
Opticianry
Optometry
Packaging Science
Paralegal Careers
Paramedical Careers
Part-time & Summer Jobs
Petroleum Careers
Pharmacy Careers
Photography
Physical Therapy Careers
Plumbing & Pipe Fitting
Podiatric Medicine
Printing Careers
Property Management
 Careers
Psychiatry
Psychology
Public Health Careers
Public Relations Careers
Purchasing Careers
Real Estate
Recreation and Leisure
Refrigeration and Air
 Conditioning Trades
Religious Service
Restaurant Careers
Retailing
Robotics Careers
Sales Careers
Sales & Marketing
Secretarial Careers
Securities Industry
Social Science Careers
Social Work Careers
Speech-Language Pathology
 Careers
Sports & Athletics
Sports Medicine

State and Local Government
Teaching Careers
Technical Communications
Telecommunications
Television and Video Careers
Theatrical Design
 & Production
Transportation Careers
Travel Careers
Veterinary Medicine Careers
Vocational and Technical
 Careers
Word Processing
Writing Careers
Your Own Service Business

CAREERS IN

Accounting
Business
Communications
Computers
Education
Engineering
Health Care
Science

CAREER DIRECTORIES

Careers Encyclopedia
Occupational Outlook Handbook

CAREER PLANNING

Handbook of Business and
 Management Careers
Handbook of Scientific and
 Technical Careers
How to Get and Get Ahead
 On Your First Job
How to Get People to Do
 Things Your Way
How to Have a Winning
 Job Interview
How to Land a Better Job
How to Prepare for College
How to Run Your Own Home
 Business
How to Write a Winning
 Résumé
Joyce Lain Kennedy's Career Book
Life Plan
Planning Your Career Change
Planning Your Career of
 Tomorrow
Planning Your College
 Education
Planning Your Military Career
Planning Your Young Child's
 Education

SURVIVAL GUIDES

High School Survival Guide
College Survival Guide

VGM Career Horizons
a division of *NTC Publishing Group*
4255 West Touhy Avenue
Lincolnwood, Illinois 60646-1975